Red Roses 'n Pinstripes

Despair to Meaning

David W. Earle, LPC

Books coauthored by David W. Earle:

Leadership - Helping others to Succeed
   with Senator George Mitchell et al.
Extreme Excellence
   with Michael Higson,Arlene R. Taylor, et al.

Books by David W. Earle:

What To Do While You Count To 10
Professor of Pain
Iron Mask
Love is Not Enough

Copyright © 2012 by David W. Earle

ISBN 13: 9781495400469

This book is dedicated:
to all those who loved and lost
to all those who loved and learned
and
to all those who love and still smile.

It is dedicated to
the generation who
someday
learns
how to love
without war.

It is dedicated
to those who will die
to those who are left behind
to those who love the dear departed
and
to those who look forward
to death
as
the
next
great
adventure.

Introduction

During the summer of 1990 in the garage of my sister's house in Sante Fe, New Mexico, I attended the first and, as far as I know, the last meeting of the Live Poets' Society.

During this visit, my teenage nephew, Jonathan Repa, and I decided to share our poetry. I was somewhat anxious in anticipation of struggling to find something positive to say about his writing. To my great surprise, his poetry was wonderful.

We had both seen the movie *The Dead Poets' Society* so we jokingly called our time in the garage, the Live Poet's Society. In this dusty garage, when we read our poetry to each other, we used this jovial play on the movie title as a "in-joke" but suddenly it came true, our sharing became alive; we discovered a wonderful way to add something unique to our literary efforts. Before we would read a poem, we would share what was going on in our lives, what feelings were occurring, what we learned from the experience, and what outcome followed. Our poetry came alive and this is book provides the powerful dimension of narrative.

A three book trilogy blossomed in my sister's garage with my nephew: *Red Roses 'n Pinstripes, Professor of Pain,* and *Iron Mask.* In these books, epic poetry and its companion narrative come alive in the manner of the Live Poets' Society. With the prose, just like in the garage with my nephew, you will experience all the pain and misery, joy and glee, sadness and heartache associated with each poem.

Professor of Pain is a collection of poetry and a self-help book or maybe a life-lesson book punctuated by poetry; when you read it, you'll have to decide. It is my journey through the perils of substance abuse with my children and my own addiction.

Iron Mask continues these snapshots into my experiences and worldview. Here, you will enjoy reading about the willingness and resistance to change, something greatly affecting our every moment. Intertwined is a maturing different view of the world occasioned by the change process. I also talk deeply about parenting and how my children affected me (They think they raised me, and, partly they did.) *Iron Mask* discusses how my parenting molded them, for good and bad; these lessons will help any parent. Then, how can any this book not include love? You will find it all in *Iron Mask.*

Red Roses 'n Pinstripes covers the hot topic of romance and its devastating companion: lost love. It is like a good war movie: a torrid romance is woven into the ravages of War and its deadly companion, Death.

Love and romance are life's adventures and their inclusion provides a gentle blanket keeping away the sharp edges of the reality of death.

These seemingly disparate topics are coupled in a unique combination where love becomes the common denominator. Break out the handkerchiefs and tissues, for *Red Roses 'n Pinstripes* promises to pull at your heart strings.

I dedicate this work to all those who played the game in love and won and for those who played and lost. If you have been on the playing field of being single and engaging in the human mating ritual, you have been or will be rejected and, in like kind, reject the advances of another for this is our natural selection dance.

In the romance section of *Red Roses 'n Pinstripes,* you will hear my lament of the loves I wanted but for some reason did not fit…the lovers I rejected and many that rejected me (can't account for poor taste).

Red Roses 'n Pinstripes is also for all those who thought about war and wondered "Why?" and have not yet come to the answer. In war, we only send our best young people who are the most physically fit, emotionally healthy, and often our most intelligent to fight the enemy's best young people. If we win, then our side has to inflict more pain and suffering upon the other side than we incurred. Winning wars requires our youth, the flowers of our nation, to make more mothers and fathers of the enemy grieve than the body bags returning home to us with a hero's welcome.

In the comics one day, the characters of Hagar the Horrible and his sidekick with the pointed hat, Lucky Eddie, were in a pitched battle. Lucky Eddie asks Hagar, 'Why do we fight so hard?' Hagar looks him in bewilderment then responded with age-old logic, "Because we are right!" The supposedly dumb sidekick then asked, "Do they fight so hard because they are wrong?"

As Pete Seeger sings, "Where have all the flowers gone?" This heart-rending song asks the same question…why? Why must we fight? Maybe "why" is not the proper question. Instead "How can we live on this planet with others who are different and discover better ways of resolving conflicts?" is the better question. "Gone to grave yards every one…when will they ever learn…when will they ever learn?"

War is the definitive adventure, ultimately bringing out the best in humans and the very worst. The Greatest Generation title should be reserved for those who come after us who figure out how to live without the physical violence of war. May they already be born.

The last section included is about death. It is dedicated to anyone who has contemplated their own demise and wondered what life is all about and the reason for this ultimate fatality. Death is a journey we all must take; we can shudder at its inevitability and try to ignore its eventuality or we can embrace what is to be and recognize it is part of the natural cycle. When fearing death, living today is missed.

Does death have meaning? Will our death mean something? A successful life includes knowing how to live, making a difference, then accepting the reality of death, and, when our time arrives, dying with grace and courage. The truth is, we will not get out of this life alive so how do we use death, our deaths, as a positive exclamation mark to our life?

Red Roses 'n Pinstripes is a disparate collection of thoughts, topics and ideas weaved together in this unique hybrid of expression to create this epic tale of loss, learning, and triumph. Are you just curious enough to see how the hero (me) fares in the end? Will his heartaches ever heal; will he ever get the girl? Can he begin to understand the ravages of war? Can this man ever understand and accept death on death's terms?

Much of what is included in this part is my own attempt to come to terms with my date with destiny, the day I discard this earthly spacesuit and collect my angel wings.

See you on the other side.

Table of Contents

Part I – Romance

Many poets write about falling in love and being carried away on a wave of bliss. Doesn't that sound wonderful and romantic? At the risk of pouring cold water on a burning heart, love is really not a feeling. Love is a decision. We choose to fall in love and/or we choose to fall out of love. Making decisions doesn't sound very romantic but this is what is happening when we get misty-eyed and crazy with love. The following section is about the decisions I made allowing myself to fall in love…time and again. Some were good decisions and some decisions were disastrous. They were all my decisions and I learned a great deal; these ladies were my teachers.

Romance combines many wonderful feelings experienced when we let down our ego-boundaries and allow our eyes to be clouded with the wonders of another person. Our hearts beat faster; colors are more intense; and we find joy where there was none. We also put up blinders to any character defects the object of our affection may have. Romantic love is the ultimate natural high of possibilities and dreams, so enjoyed when present and so missed when it departs.

Expressing who we are in conjunction with another is the Noah's Ark Syndrome: two by two we march on this earth, each to discover ourselves in relationship with another. Mother Nature provides this illusion of perfection to propagate the earth with more humans; yes, being all goo-goo eyed is Mother Nature's way of having babies. However, no other area provides the rich vein of self-knowledge than in a close relationship. And no other area is so fraught with pain nor as rewarding as love.

Falling in love is easy. Staying in love is difficult. In this section, I talk about the experiences when I lose my breath and often my good senses in romance, where I throw caution out the window, discount past hurts and disappointments, and fall in love… again. In this section, love is the romance I so piously covet, but when it ends, the grief becomes my constant companion. So for the moment, enjoy the blissful pounding of this poet's heart as I plunge headlong into the fog and mysteries of love.

Sworn to Honesty

Honesty is one of the most valuable commodities in a relationship; it is also very rare. In the poems Sworn to Honesty and Fidelity Trust Bank, the lovers protect themselves from the fear of getting hurt. They hide who they really are behind a protective mask of dishonesty, thinking this mask will defend them from what hurts most - reality. They assume they don't have to be vulnerable and let someone in, yet it is intimacy they seek. Maybe this assumption is out of ignorance or, more than likely, out of the fear of being vulnerable.

Intimacy is what we all crave in a significant, romantic relationship and sexual intimacy is part of this equation. However, there are other forms of intimacy. There is intellectual intimacy, where when we work on a project, each person's view and suggestions are validated and considered. There is physical intimacy, where we can connect with a physical touch, hug, or handshake, a connection made with no link with sex.

Then, there is emotional intimacy. Couples get together for emotional intimacy, for both want to substantially connect to another human and feel closer to their chosen one than anyone else in the entire world. They want their significant other to be there for them, to struggle to understand them, to accept them as they are and not demand change. They want their significant other to believe in them. They want these people to know them profoundly, yet it is often the fear of this intimate knowledge keeping them separate from what they want most.

Intimacy is broken down into two parts: the first part is, *see* and the second, *into me*...as in *see-into-me*. Couples desperately want this connection but are afraid to invest their honesty in its achievement. Without this profound connection, couples are not getting what they bargained for and often blame their partner for this disconnection. Deep down, many of their arguments are based upon this basic requirement of this unexpressed and often

11

unacknowledged desire they have yet achieved. Usually, this lack is so fundamental and so deep many people are unaware of the real reason for their unhappiness.

In Sworn to Honesty and Fidelity Trust Bank, two lovers hide behind their masks but still think the love they so ardently desire will happen without the necessary ingredient of vulnerability. They are amazed when love fails. What they want most – the intimacy of having one person know the depths of their souls and still accepting them as they are – to know their partner loves them despite their warts. These wishes become an impossibility without honesty. This couple superficially goes through the motions of love where this denial becomes an illusion which will ultimately shatter their relationship. For without the foundation of honesty, how can they build a good foundation?

How can couples achieve this vital part of the magic of intimacy unless there is honesty? They push away what they want most, the possibility of deep love. The truth of this equation…love is not enough. In my book, *Love is Not Enough*, explores what happens when love is not enough and how to increase the effectiveness of our love.

Sworn to Honesty

Two perfect lovers ... sworn to honesty
            to be intimate ... complete understanding
            eye to eye they smile
            hour after hour, revealing themselves.
            They know each other so well.

They each look so sweet ... behind their masks
            saying what will not offend
            walking on egg-shells ... not being honest,
            you know, for the sake of the relationship.

Don't want to rock the boat.
            Don't reveal ... Don't let someone in.
            This boat is too shaky and we might drown.
            Real honesty might hurt feelings.

He turned to his best friend, Bill -
            "She's never on time; it pisses me off."
            "Please excuse my being late," she says.
            "It's okay, I know you're busy," he responds.

She turned to her best friend across the street
            "I care for him a lot.
            I think I care more for him than he does for me;
            I mustn't let him know or I might get hurt."
            Don't risk ... Don't be vulnerable.

To Bill, he says:
            "I'm afraid she is not really interested in me.
            Maybe she likes me
            however, she has so many other men friends.
            She must like our relationship just the way it is."

Don't let her know your true feelings.
　　Don't let her know the truth.
　　To Bill he says:
　　"My job is the pits, but I'm afraid of losing it."

"How's your job doing, sweetie?" she asks
　　"Oh, fine, you know … same old same old."

　What? Let her know of my fears?
　What? Let him know the real me?
　　Are you kidding?
　　Sworn to honesty …
　　to be intimate … complete understanding
　　… two perfect lovers.

Fidelity Trust Bank

The radio announcer declared

"Store your emotions in
      Fidelity Trust Bank.
      Your feelings are insured,
      guaranteed never to be hurt again."

"Don't invest who you are
      by risking it on life's uncertainties."

"Keep it locked safe inside
      these solid high walls
      of iron and concrete."

Being a smart investor
      she locked all
      her emotions, fears, and feelings
      safely inside this stately old bank.

Living in fear
I couldn't tell you … had to hide,
      for if you really knew me,
      I might not be enough
          … and this is all I have.

Words echoed in his being
      "She doesn't trust …
      She doesn't trust … Me."

And at the end of the day,
a street cleaner picks up
a discarded mask.

A beautiful mask,
now replaced with another
once proudly worn
by a young lady
who banks at Fidelity Trust.

With his own Fidelity Trust passbook
safely tucked in his pocket,
a tired man mutters to himself
his voice echoing within his mask
       "She doesn't trust …
       She doesn't trust …Me."

No one was listening.
No one knew how to be honest.

She Called Me

One night, I met a woman who brought sparkles to my eyes. God did an excellent job of designing this lady before me, and I trembled with excitement when close to her. We talked several times and I was about to ask her out when the red flags started waving and I decided I could not afford the maintenance a relationship with her would cost.

She Called Me is a recognition of my hard won ability to reject, in spite of physical desire, those who have high maintenance personalities and a price tag I was no longer willing to finance.

She Called Me

She called
me …
Dear.

She
called
me …
Love

My aching heart, I fear

this new beauty in my life

is
rather
insincere.

Crowd of a Few

Crowd of a Few is another metaphor about flying to gain spirituality. In this poem, I am the jilted lover whose death wish is overcome with the stark reality that this life's journey is individual, personal, and in my case can be only achieved by me, not with anyone…no matter how special…just me. Before my crash and burn from the skies, I discovered a spiritual connection when my thinking changed.

As an anonymous songwriter wrote words much better than I and George Jones sings:
> "You gotta walk this lonesome valley
> And you gotta walk, walk it by yourself
> Nobody here can walk it for you
> You gotta walk, walk it by yourself".

Crowd of a Few is this quest for a spiritual lost love and finding the ultimate truth.

Crowd of a Few

We flew together dodging dark clouds
then soaring towards the sun.
Alone you flew into a cloud
as white as winter's snow flakes
to my amazement, you were flying away!
My shouts were to no avail.

Wind in my face,
my screams died in my throat
only echoing wind's angry rush
the tiny figure you'd become.

Your tear-stained face suddenly became clear
and with a still voice,
whispered on the wind,
"It's better this way."

My wings lost their strength.
I fell toward earth,
wind's rush against my face
gathering speed, life-disregarding-plunge.
Echoing through my being
"It's better this way"
vibrates my aching head.
My broken heart now leads the way.

Gazing towards the on rushing earth
what she said was true …
My wings then took me upward,
skyward to the blackness of space.

To leave this earthly existence
to where man's spirit mingles with creativity
this is a journey I must take on my own …
not hand-in-hand as imagination dreamed.

Relentless quest for truth
in a crowd of a few
to know all that I am …
to touch the face of God.

One Day Last Summer

Timing of a successful, committed relationship is often a vital component determining if the relationship continues or becomes a washed out remembrance of faded photographs and treasured movie stubs. In the middle of my mid-life crisis, I met someone who inspired me, but we both knew…I was not ready for a committed relationship.

One Day Last Summer is about one such important learning experience; we both understood the reason and it was sad when our love faded into just a memory.

One Day Last Summer

We danced in the sunshine
on a summer's day …
an afternoon in the park.

Round 'n round
Laughing 'n smiling
completely aware of each other.

As the band played
our favorite songs,
we danced fast then slow.

Each of us knowing the afternoon
would someday end,
wishing it would last forever.

We tried to forget …
closing our eyes to the truth
tomorrow would ever come.

In one fleeting moment
we stole a kiss,
an embrace for a lifetime.

And in the cool of summer's eve,
the band played the last song
as we held each other tight.

At the last rays of the day,
we left the park
hand 'n hand we silently walked.

At the corner she kissed my cheek
and smiled, "I'll see you tomorrow."
I nodded my head as my heart pounded.

She turned and walked toward home,
as I watched her disappear
in the horizon of summer's shadows.

One day last summer,
we shared a moment in life
with all the intensity available.

Just a moment in our lives
we shared together, now only a memory
… one day last summer.

Embraced with White Lace

On the surface, Embraced with White Lace might seem very sexually suggestive. In addition to its provocative imagery, there is a deeper message of how significant relationships present distinct possibilities for deep self-understanding and self-acceptance.

Embraced with White Lace asks the question "Must I unwrap another and then another before this promise of self-discovery is to be mine?" The answer was "yes" for me, for several more beauties would be required before I would be ready to meet the woman who I would marry. Had I not had these experiences and learned these needed lessons before I met Penny, I would have not be the man she needed and she would have rejected me like many before.

I thank you, my "White Laced Beauty," for helping me to get ready for a more mature form of love.

Embraced with White Lace

White shining paper, neatly wrapped box
I know it contains something very special.
Bright pink ribbon,
embraced with white lace
adorns this box making it a beauty to behold.
This beautiful covering hides the magic within,
The promise of excitement,
the wonder of the unknown.

As I ponder the contents
of this box I hold in my hands
I quiver with the question,
what is hidden within?

Time slowly reveals the answer.
This box is for me
a gift of all my possibilities.
My capacity to love deeply as never before,
the trust to allow someone to love me,
to let another enter the very depths of my being.

You are the beautiful wrapping
adoring this package.
It must be opened
before my treasure is revealed.
Will I obtain my gifts in your arms?
Or is there another within this box
adorned with someone else's colors?
Must I unwrap another and then another
before this promise is to be mine?

If I want to learn to love
then I must risk,
to have trust.

For a heart full of fear cannot begin to love.

As I gently tug on this ribbon
removing the outer wrapping
I tremble with excitement.
What gifts are held within this box
bright pink ribbon
embraced with white lace?

Dumpster's Shade

When a friend and I would go to lunch often the only parking place available was next to the dumpster. We laughed about how many times our lunch started off with the unappetizing aroma only found with refuse.

This particular trash dumpster had all the many multitudes of fragrant smells and all the assortment of flies one could imagine. We made jokes about how this dumpster affected our romance.

Dumpster's Shade was the result of my aromatic humor but without the stench of a dumpster.

Dumpster's Shade

In the summer heat
by the ole steel dumpster
you 'n I fell deeply in love.

You looked so sweet to me
in your faded overalls …
a pink ribbon in your hair.

And in the dumpster's shade
we'd share a meal together
'till the noon whistle blew.

Moon pies, tater chips,
Hershey Bars, 'n RC Cola
all the food groups
you covered so well.

With a roar 'n a mighty back-fire,
you'd park your chopper cycle
in defiance of the handicapped zone.

"Emotionally handicapped"
Was your gibe reframed,
very funny … and oh, so true.

I looked into your brown eyes,
kissed your soft hands,
then cleaned the grease
from under your nails.

You always called me "darling"
even when you're mad
"Damn it, darling!" often echoed
from your lovely ruby lips.

Today, I cannot pass a dumpster,
'n smell deeply of its aroma
without remembering you, my love.

You are
the greatest love
a man could ever have …
With my name tattooed
upon your chest …
could any man ask for more?

In Touch with Forever

A friend helped me develop personal boundaries. With her, I developed a deep friendship and although this closeness was part of our relationship, we kept it at that, friendship. At this time in my life, it was important for me to learn to appreciate her as person without the complexity of passion.

At this time, we both needed physical connection, understanding, and friendship but nothing more was in the cards. I developed a warm, close friendship with this woman, who in the eyes of the world (and mine) was very beautiful. We chose not to complicate our friendship with love; instead, we agreed on a significant friendship and here another lesson was learned.

In Touch with Forever celebrates this wonderful friendship.

In Touch with Forever

Total acceptance
warmth of another
held close in my arms
experiencing a time extended hug ...
suspended dimension.

I felt her closeness
our separateness vague
no talking ... no movement
only contact ... body contact
feels warms ... secure.

Her breast is pressing on my chest
romantic but strangely non arousing
mutual touch non-sexual
was stimulated and
amplified by emotional warmth.

Valued friendship
special type of friend
transcends societies' understanding.

Held in total trust
acceptance of personal boundaries
our mental barriers melted
disappearing in this moment.

Our emotions were combined
with mutual needs
of acceptance and warmth.

A glimpse of heaven
total contact with the moment
mood altering experience,
what we both were needing.

A higher level of conscience
being held in total trust
total acceptance of another
secure and warm.

Special friendship
No expectations .... No demands
... in touch with forever.

Circles and Triangles

In 1989 to 1991 I was a member of the Broadmoor Church Singles Group called "Celebrations." Circles and Triangles is a spoof on this experience; the names and identities have been changed to protect the most vulnerable and the many friendships I gained from this exciting time during my mid-life crisis.

In this poem, I poke fun at the many complex intricacies happening in the tides and cross-tides of the playing field of being single.

Note: With the cell phone technology of today, the reference to "pagers" is antiquated but hopefully the symbolism will not be lost.

Circles and Triangles

I love an oncology nurse named, Inez, and it grieves me so,
for she loves only Fred, a commercial real estate appraiser.
Now Fred is charming, witty but he's also chasing Mary,
who owns a florist shop, but, I hear, is making it with a chemical
engineer named Mike.

Mike wears a pager everywhere he goes … to impress single women.
He acts free and easy but has not forgotten in his ex-wife, Ann
who loves her new job as a bug exterminator.

Charlie saw how impressed the women were by Mike's pager.
Since he didn't have one, he hung a garage door opener on his belt at
the last dance, was teased unmercifully, and hasn't been back to a
function since.

Jennifer, an executive sales secretary, fell head over heels for John
on their second date. John travels for a contractor, estimating or
something.

John falls in love four times a year and with each season's change
he'll be grieving the lost of his latest love writing poetry lamenting
that loss, and looking forward to the next season.

Samantha, the pain therapist, thinks John would make someone else
very happy and cannot explain why she's not interested in John,
which is the pattern of John's love-life.

John's latest love, Belinda, lifts weights to keep trim and as we
observe still is, will always love Sam, the college archivist.
She would run off to Rio with him but is fearful how her stretch
marks would look on naked beaches.

Roy, a newspaper printer for seventeen years and Samantha were
high school sweethearts. However, Roy thinks she's hung up on
John...we know she is not. Samantha would not tell Roy how she
really feels about him ... she doesn't want him to get the upper hand.

Sam, while waiting for Belinda to return from the travel agency
had his town house exterminated
and met the girl of his dreams, Ann.

Inez, while waiting in line for yogurt at the health food store,
met a guy, named Charlie, who loves electronic gadgets
and ever since they've been spending weekends
in the French Quarter.
No wonder we haven't seen him.

Are you confused? Bewildered?
Well, so are the singles who
        live in this real life soap opera.
                Tell me, with all this happening ...
                        why would anyone watch daytime TV?

The Heart Speaks

The day I moved out of my home and into the world of being single, that night I went to my first singles' party. I did not want to be alone in that barren apartment all by myself. I was needy, very needy.

At that party, I met the woman I'd be in a relationship with for the next 14 months. She was somebody I desperately needed at the time and that relationship taught a great many lessons.

Many people I met at this party became good friends. Later on I had a discussion with one of these friends concerning remarriage. Her wise advice was to take four years before trying it again. This is sound advice and, if followed, decreases the possibilities of rebound marriage. Hopefully, with significant time, the person learns the lessons so necessary for a successful relationship, for remember…love is not enough. The conversation then turned and she talked about what she saw in me, "You will not last four years."

In my arrogance, I thought she just gave me a compliment. I assumed that I was such a good catch, so many women would be interested in me that I would be overwhelmed with possibilities. I would get the number one draft choice for that year! I realized later that her comment was not a compliment. It was directed at me because it was obvious to my new friends, I was so wounded, and so needy that I would latch onto the first person who smiled at me. My new love was a perfect example of my need to connect with someone and fill my abandonment needs.

I attended a divorce adjustment seminar in the fall of 1989 and the instructor made a vivid illustration describing the neediness I felt. "Picture a group of needy singles at a dance," she told us, "all with their umbilical cords out and swinging it around over their heads ready to lasso someone." How true this was for me, I just lassoed the first one who smiled at me.

She and I made a perfect couple. I was needy and she needed someone to fix, a reclamation endeavor, a construction project, someone to focus on so she would not have to work on herself. I fit the bill. I was the stray puppy she always wanted, muddy paws and all. I would spend the next fourteen months with her, seven months getting into the relationship and then seven months getting out of it. She turned out to be a good person who taught me a lot and I am so grateful for that experience. I think she will admit I also taught her many lessons.

I wrote, The Heart Speaks, soon after meeting this new person. Here are my thoughts and fears when I realized I was in another relationship so soon after ending one. Recognize my unwavering uncertainty, wounded heart, and complete denial of current reality.

Thank god, my lasso broke and we didn't marry. I know now, our relationship was a train wreck about to happen, another failed relationship.

The Heart Speaks

What is a risk worth?:
When to gamble? When to run?
My old love is gone leaving a large void,
the hurt creates a vacuum in my heart.
>Anything to fill the hole.
>Anything not to hurt.

First one you meet, first one who cares
Void is filled. I don't feel the pain.
What are the chances this new love is real?
Too soon...Too quick...Too intense.
Violates rules of logic.

Intellect rejects, passion embraces...heart hesitates.
Let's reject, let's not be hurt.
Don't gamble the remaining undamaged heart fibers.

And yet...
>Here she comes.
>Hear her laugh.
>Feel her warmth.

Is she the love you wanted
or destruction about to happen?
Intellect rejects, passion embraces ... the heart vacillates.
To commit is not smart... rejection does not fit.
Draw to an inside straight? Against the odds.

The heart now speaks, feeble from its wounds
I listen.
>"Never again can the warmth disappear."
>"Never again can the touch be taken."
>>I listen.

And yet …
>Here she comes.
>Hear her laugh.
>Feel her warmth.

"What the hell?" The heart says,
"Maybe we can survive."

Intellect slams the door in anger!
Passions cheers.
The heart just prays.

Yet to Meet

After spending the summer licking my wounds from my last relationship (see Magnolia's Blossom), I thought I might be ready for a more significant relationship. I wrote Yet to Meet when I decided to prepare myself for the opportunity of when a committed relationship could become a possibility.

At the end of August, 1990, right after I wrote this poem, I met Penny, the woman I would ultimately marry. I discovered she was also working hard, learning how to trade chaos for peace, control for acceptance, and discord for love. It was serendipity when I discovered she had the same desires as I.

Red Roses 'n Pinstripes and Princess of Pleasure are the romance poems I wrote with a big grin while in the throes of new love. She was like no one I had ever met and I am so glad I was ready to meet her when I did.

Yet to Meet

Here's to you,
whom I've yet to meet.
Your spiritual presence
has proceeded your arrival.
"Tis true, I know, you're on your way."

My heat awakens at your image,
for only it knows what to expect.
You name has not dwelled
upon my lips; yet, I know you well.

I have seen your face
in my fellow human beings …
as they struggle to become.
I feel your tender skin
when I touch a soul in need.

We know each other well,
for we have travelled
many the same skyways.

The essence of creation
we have come to learn …
for we have been tempered by life,
discovered the blue pearl of serenity
within our souls.

We share a passion for living
pursuing the quest for beauty.
Each possessing an internal peace
which is far … far beyond happiness.

With love for our Creator,
His will as a commandment
two independent souls
hand in hand will journey
this life together.

You already exist,
I feel it …
we've just
yet to be introduced.
Let's talk

.

Epilogue: Yet to Meet

Penny and I were married on October 24, 1991 and I am so glad I was ready for this magnificent woman.

After my editor made suggestions for changes, ~~then~~ I again reviewED the proof and finally asked Penny to do her magic. She is very good at finding grammatically ERROR~~y~~ incorrect words, typos, misspellings, and insists on addition OR precision WITH ~~on~~ what I thought was already finished. Without her input, my writing would lack the clarity I desire for my readers. We used this pattern on three books before this one. However, this book, as you are discovering, is different.

Penny read all of these poems before she started to edit this book, but the magnitude of all my past loves collected together became difficult for any spouse to take. She told me how hard this book was for her to read; yet she did. She knew how much I wanted to express myself through this book so she edited for me. I felt loved.

When you finish this book it is Penny you really need to thank. If she told me she did not want this book published, it would not have been.

Double Jointed Lover

Because of the obvious implications expressed in the poem, Double Jointed Lover, the identity of this person will only be known to me and the double jointed lover.

Here's to you, my *double jointed lover*!

Double Jointed Lover

Long and lovely legs
pretty woman, movie star
in the tub with her lover
all bubbles and smiles.
In soap and suds, my lover
makes Pretty Woman seem tame
when she wraps her legs 'round me,
my *double joined lover*.

Bo Derrick, a perfect ten
a body to behold
eye of men's delight
beyond imagination's raptures.
In the eye of the beholder
a perfect ten I know
when surrounded by the legs of
my *double joined lover*.

Flying arrows and mighty swords
a giant horse of deceit
long ago war fought for a woman
the lovely Helen of Troy.
A battle is raging in my heart
my soul's consumed by fire
with her legs 'round my being
my *double joined lover*.

The famous Mona Lisa
leaves her haunting smile
forever etched in a heart
just waiting to be returned.
All smiles am I
in the loving caresses
a tender scissor-lock from
my *double joined lover*

Red Roses 'n Pinstripes

I got the idea for the name of this poem from a bar at the foot of Esplanade Avenue in New Orleans; the bar was called Pinstripes 'n Black Lace. It was a bar I would not ever frequent but I loved the name.

When struck dumb with love for my soon to be bride, Red Roses 'n Pinstripes is my howling at the moon in sheer delight.

Red Roses 'n Pinstripes

Witness the birth of a dream:
Red roses 'n Pinstripes.
Pinstripes 'n Black Lace.

Two lovers wished upon a star
then threw different coins
into the
same fountain,
combining
two separate dreams
by two lost dreamers.

A dream nurtured 'n gently held
by two dreamers,
then wished
into possibilities.

Red roses 'n pinstripes.
Pinstripes 'n black lace.
A dream dancing
in night visions
which melts
by anticipation
and then kissed
into possibilities
by yonder star.

The beginning of a dream,
the start of an adventure
of romance ...
Red roses 'n pinstripes.
Pinstripes 'n black lace.

Princess of Pleasure

The Creator made all humans sexual creatures and by design…life is sexually transmitted. This was not done out of malice or a warped sense of humor but because this connection is so powerful, it creates a method of knowing another person in many profound experiences: emotionally, spiritually, and sexually. This connection provides a way to express ourselves with deep feelings in this love affirming process; it is also good for creating babies.

In this close relationship, I discovered a wonderful paradox in enjoying someone in a mutually loving and fulfilling sexual relationship, another connection beyond the emotional and sexual act itself. Love making creates one of the tremendous opportunity to increase a spiritual connection with our creator.

The poem, Princess of Pleasure, is accepting the beauty of a sexual relationship; accepting myself my Creator made me – a sexual being; and then the realization that this closeness is much more than physical. In the right circumstances, in a loving committed relationship, a sexual connection is an act of worship.

Princess of Pleasure

As I search for my own spirituality
I discover a paradox,
a direct connection with my own sexuality
and the god spirit
which lives deep within my soul.

"Teach me, my tiger" she softly sings
"how to love you ... teach me tonight."

Her warm breath in my ear;
hot passion in my jeans.
The touch of her tongue
melts all my resistance.

Princess of Pleasure -
white lace 'n silk, depth of her eyes
thousand twinkling stars
on a snowy cold night.

In birthday suit pajamas,
my inhibitions removed.
All sense of time distorted
until naked first touched.
I yield myself to thee.

And in bed sheet castles
kings and queens are we
hands touching bodies
soft satin 'n fingertips.
Contentment beyond the cat's purr.

I am your prisoner -
captive of your charm
perfume prison bars
keeps me locked
deep within your soul.

My desire is to express
this part of my being
as an act of worship.

Singing praises to my creator
who gave to me this powerful gift
as a celebration
of His love.

Epilogue: Princess of Pleasure

Acknowledgement: The lyrics "Teach me tiger how to love you ... teach me tonight" is borrowed from the song by Sharon M. Draper entitled *Teach Me Tiger* and sung in different renditions by both April Stevens and Marilyn Monroe.

I first heard *Teach Me Tiger* in the spring 1964, while I was attending Sam Houston State University in Huntsville, Texas. One evening I received an anonymous phone call. Someone called me by name and played *Teach Me Tiger* sung by April Stevens over the telephone. I had never heard that song before and the sexy voice and suggestive lyrics set my 19 year old, already high testosterone level into absolute orbit.

Whoever played it to me never acknowledged the call; I think this mysterious girl must have enjoyed my frantic panting for *Teach Me Tiger* is the sexiest song ever sung to a love-starved teenager. It was so memorable; I immediately bought the record and began reliving that exciting moment.

Princess of Pleasure takes over where *Teach Me Tiger* left off.

Remembering Love Lost

If you are on the playing field of being single, you are playing a game…the game of love. In this adventure, you will constantly reject others and be rejected, such are results of the brutal game. Love is not for the weak at heart.

Looking for love is like buying a suit of clothes. You walk into the store and look for your size, rummage through the various colors and styles, and then pick one that you like. If it appeals to you enough, you try it on. Some you may like, but then discover something you don't like even before trying it on, discarding it on a whim of preference. Others, you might even try on and like incredibly well, but when you notice the price, "Oh, this one costs too much" you say to yourself as you put it back on the rack.

As you experience different suits, some fit better than others but none are striking enough to wear for the rest of your life, so you go to another store and repeat the cycle. Even after finding the perfect suit, you may discover that you are just not ready or don't have the necessary cash and lay-away may be too painful an option.

The complex part of this analogy is that while you are making your selection, contrary to a real department store, these suits are also trying you on, being as fussy as you are, and sometimes rejecting the "perfect" suit you planned on purchasing. Harry Potter would be most comfortable with suits being able to choose people but no matter how often humans participate, this rejecting and being rejected is hard on the heart and evokes pain. Welcome to romance - get used to it!

From my own experience, I learned a lot getting into a relationship, continued learning during the courtship, and gained even more wisdom when the relationship ended. From the poems found in Part II – Love Lost, you will read me lamenting the agony of the rejection and the guilt when rejecting another.

Knowing all those wonderful gifts of learning are packaged with pain, ultimately, becomes bearable when the opportunity for learning is realized.

So get out your handkerchief, grab a box of tissues, and join me in the adventures of my lost loves.

Broken Hearted Sidewalk

I was in Lynchburg, Virginia visiting my parents when I saw my young niece drawing on the sidewalk. Her mother and dad had just split up and I knew this was affecting the entire family. As I looked over her shoulder, I was not prepared to read this child-like hieroglyphics written in chalk on my parent's sidewalk.

Broken Hearted Sidewalk is about one sad, young girl, desperately trying to make sense about her loss of mommy and daddy together, a situation about which she had no control but required her to pay a terrible price.

Broken Hearted Sidewalk

Chalk on the sidewalk
drawn on the concrete.

Daddy doesn't live here anymore.

A nine year old
drew herself
in chalk …
artistically inaccurate
but an emotional
encyclopedia.

Daddy doesn't live here anymore.

She drew a sad little girl
with exaggerated features …
an unhappy expression.

And within this chalk person
drawn on a sidewalk
the image of a heart
which is
obviously
broken.

For the sidewalk artist
draws what she is feeling
… broken-hearted fears

Daddy doesn't live here anymore.

Future, Warmth, and Touch

In 1987, when my 20-year marriage ended, I experienced a great deal of emotional pain. During that same time frame, someone gave me a tool to help with the emotional distress. Before recovery, I would have turned to my mistress, "Ethel" ... as in ethyl-alcohol. Alcohol would have numbed the pain, at least temporarily.

In the midst of the rejection from a 20-year mate, I needed some help to manage this painful awareness. I knew alcohol wasn't the solution, but "What could I do?" Fortunately, someone gave me something that worked much better; a method to heal instead of a place to hide: "When the grief threatens to overwhelm you during the day and you have difficulty doing your job, make a date with yourself for that evening to have a personal grief session. If you make this date, it is critical you actually show up when you said you would." For lack of a better term, have your own private *pity party*.

When I heard this wise counsel, I didn't think I would need it. As life unfolds, shortly thereafter, in mid-October 1987, I was in Mexico doing a very difficult business assignment. The three weeks of that experience could evolve into an exciting chapter by itself, but for the purpose of this book, those secrets shall remain in my memory.

My wife of 20 years had separated from me in September and I was still reeling from her rejection. I found myself on the Mexican side of the border in a room full of strangers speaking Spanish, a language I did not speak. I felt very alone and isolated. In the middle of these intense business negations, the separation pain and sadness hit me and these strong emotions were distracting me from the concentration necessary for this business deal. I felt like crying right in the middle of the meeting, a very inappropriate thing, especially considering all the machismo in the room.

During this meeting in Mexico, I was feeling choked up with emotions. I stuffed those feelings and promised a date that night with myself for my own private grief session. Once I made this agreement, the emotions lost their grip on me for they realized that now I would listen to them. That evening feeling so alone, isolated, rejected, and miserable I went back to the little Mexican motel and dealt with my anguish. I followed this friend's advice. For three nights in a row, I had my own *pity party.*

I allowed myself grief sessions where I rolled on the floor, got a snotty nose, and threw up in the commode. What I was doing was managing grief. Instead of allowing the grief to control me, I was now managing my sorrow. I didn't stuff it, ignore it, or fail to respond to its call, but when it demanded my attention, I heard it's voice and using this method I was able to manage my grief.

Healthy people manage strong emotions for hiding or ignoring these emotions requires a terrible price. It can be equally debilitating when a person allows their emotions to control them. What is healthy is to manage emotions, not run from, not ignore their power, nor allow these feelings to be in control. Having your own personal *pity-party* is a wonderful tool for successfully managing grief. What I did in the little Mexican Hotel those nights so long ago was manage my sorrow, depression, and grief. Having your own pity party is an effective method for managing loss.

After the second night of my *pity-party*, knowing I needed a third, I decided to write down what I was experiencing. These painful sessions ultimately unleashed an avalanche of poetry, some of which you are now reading. Future, Warmth, and Touch comes from the personal notes I made during the third night when again I met myself in grief.

Those notes written in bitter anguish are an expression of honest, raw feelings that would launch my poetry career. Tell me now, did the poetry flowing from my private *pity-party* add or detract from the world's finest literature? You be the judge.

Future, Warmth, and Touch

After a while you run out of excuses
    You must return to your room.
    You must face reality.

Reality awaits
    lifts his head and bows as you enter
    no TV, newspaper, phone
    no escape from your appointment
    with reality.

The radio is playing
    songs of love
    melodies bring back memories
    some painful, some happy.

Reality stares at you and chants:
    "You are alone."
    "You are rejected"
    "You are worthless."
    "You have no future, warmth, nor touch!"

No smiles, no love, only pain ... severe pain.
    Tears fall as reality speaks.
    Tears fall as I listen.
    Tears fall as I believe.
    Tears fall as I slowly die in rejection.
No smiles, no love, only pain ... severe pain.

Tears fall on the page as I write
    and yet with every word, reality starts to fade.
Sunlight enters my room
    bringing light not hope
    bringing warmth not promises.
Feel the pain ... cry the tears
    allowing it all to escape.

Only then can I be well.
Only then can I begin again.

The tears come packaged with the pain
            washes out some of the hurt
            making room for growth
            gathering of inner strength.

To love myself ... To respect myself.
To face reality and declare:
            I am not alone .... not rejected ... not worthless
                    I have me!
            I do have future, warmth, and touch
                    I now have me!

Professor of Pain

In *Future, Warmth, and Touch*, I wrote about the wisdom of having a personal pity party to manage grief. This is a coping skill I used several times since those painful nights in Mexico. Now, when I find it necessary to have a *pity-party*, I add something to this coping skill by personifying the emotional pain and call the grief, "Professor," as in *Professor of Pain*. Somehow, having a name for my grief makes it more manageable and less frightening. The Professor then becomes a companion, someone who is there to help me work through the suffering and to find meaning in the loss.

I use this poem as a therapeutic tool for grieving clients. I suggest they invite the Professor to their pity-party; somehow his presence provides comfort during these high trauma moments experienced in these grief sessions.

Professor of Pain is also included in the two the previous books. This is not an error for it fits so nicely into the topics of the Professor of Pain and Iron Mask that I included it again in this one. Visiting the Professor is such a powerful concept, I think it needs inclusion any time life throws us a curve ball and we experience loss, suffering, sadness, and need to grieve.

Understand in the midst of your pain, the measure of your grief is a measure of your depth of caring. If you did not care, why grieve? Say hello to the Professor of Pain for me; he and I know each other very well. As said in the poem, "Pain is a part of living" and we can either accept the reality of the loss or be consumed by the intensity of the pain.

The grief process is about the journey from denial to our current reality, whether we like this reality or not …it is what it is. When in dark despair and depression is sitting heavily on your chest, the Professor is willing to be your guide towards the light.

All you have to do is invite him in.

Professor of Pain

The large steel doors slowly opened.
A sinister professor dressed in long black robes
smiled and bowed, as I entered.
His smile was returned by me, then the bow
and to his great surprise ... a hug!
The hard lines on his face
became suddenly softer, gentler, even fatherly.
"You gave me an embrace?"
"You gave me knowledge."
I went to the front of the classroom,
took a front row seat, awaiting his lecture.
For a moment in silence he pondered,
he sat at the edge of his desk
looking at me over his bifocals.

"You embraced me, the Professor of Pain!"
"Yes, sir, I respect you."
"Do you know who I am?"
"You're on the payroll; you are on my side."

A large grin appeared on his face.
"You have just passed your final exam.
You have now graduated.
What are your plans my son?"
"I came here to celebrate life.
You are part of living;
I want to continue my education."
He took off his robe ...
a glow came over his head
his angel wings were exposed,
he looked at me, winked, and spoke:
"You can now see me as I am;
underclassman are not allowed to know."
He shuffled his papers,
cleared his throat, and began to lecture

Memory in a Glass Decanter

Shortly after I wrote this poem, I received from the object of my
affections, her rejection letter, a true *Dear John*, only my letter
said "Dear David". This poem has not a hint of the disaster
looming over the horizon, and from my ignorance, her letter
totally blindsided me. You will read more about the rejection letter
in the next poem after this one entitled: *Tears Fell*.

Reading *Memory in a Glass Decanter,* you know what I did not
know at that time. However, for now, enjoy the blissful moment
this poem has to tell.

Memory in a Glass Decanter

A memory to cherish
like a fine wine
now mellowed with age ...
old friends now brand new.

A memory in a glass decanter
to be held to the light
enjoying the bouquet
aroma of a caring friend
savored and enjoyed.

Asleep in my arms
your head upon my chest
indelibly imprinting
this moment deep in my heart.
Last morning of a very few
we shared together
feeling acceptance
contentment ... complete trust.

The memory is deep in my heart
holding you in my arms,
smell of your hair,
touch of your skin.
Today's silver carpet
will return you to a world
of tall buildings ...to a beginning never to end.

Your parting was not misery
for you have given me a great gift ...
shared happy moments, a moment in time.

A faint fragrance
lingered in my room
a reminder of you ...
a memory in a glass decanter.

Tears Fell

I warned you about my "Dear John" letter. This is the only one I
ever experienced and hope never to receive another. Tears Fell is
about the written announcement I received from a girlfriend after
she returned to Virginia. I received this "Dear John" letter
informing me our relationship no longer included me,
This announcement was sudden, for I thought our love would
grow into something beautiful. I lacked the awareness of what
caused this sudden, shocking decision or maybe she was not
honest with me before she left. The net result was this letter and
the emotions it caused.

She never told me the reason for her rejection. The reason must
have been hidden somewhere in the obscure bottom of her heart,
but all I had was rejection's pain. As the reality became clearer,
the feelings of rejection increased as her reasons faded into
obscurity and became unimportant.

Tears Fell relives this one day when reality hit, and it was not what
I wanted it to be.

Tears Fell

A birth of romance
beauty to behold.
Who knows what promises
are to be enjoyed.

Romance suddenly ends
with a haunting question
... a wisp of smoke
a shadow which eludes
all who question.
No satisfactory
answer of knowing
for the heart has reasons
which eludes the mind of man.

Tears fell on the page as she wrote.
Tears fell on the page as I read.
The reason why is just a whisper
on the lips of gods and angels.

The turning of the world
will continue the sun will rise tomorrow
        "... and the Lord is
        close to the brokenhearted."
Two hearts cry the same mournful song

... Why? Why? Why?

Each knowing the reason is not important.
Tears fell on the page as she wrote.
Tears fell on the page as I read.

Two hearts who once touched
        came close
        and now somehow
        are not.

Epilogue – Tears Fell:

Just before the publishing of this book, I attended my 50th class reunion of E. C. Glass High School in Lynchburg, Virginia. (It was really my classmates' 50th reunion as I could not be that old!) I had a great time visiting with my many friends and about a half-dozen told me it was obvious I had more fun than anyone. I think they were right!

At our reunion, my Tears Fell friend was there. This was the first time I had seen her in 23 years. What was rewarding was the warm hug she gave me and then she told me why her tears stained the pages when she wrote the Dear John letter so long ago letting me go. She then made her amends for what happened. We both felt a great release and were thankful for the long delayed closure.

Fear's Yoke

People have come into my life and although they are unaware of their effect, they often teach me a wonderful life-lesson. Lessons are the necessary building blocks toward maturity, a state I successfully resisted until the fear of change was overcome the misery of status quo.

Fear's Yoke and *Songs of Love* are about one such person and the lessons she unknowingly taught me - important experiences, painfully learned.

Fear's Yoke

In the quiet of early dawn,
Sunday morning shining down
these thoughts I have of you:
white bunny pin
holes in my pockets
white chocolate mousse
pink tooth brush
yellow squash 'n zucchini
muffins and raisins
teddy bears 'n more teddy bears.
Things that remind me of you.

The beauty I will remember
what was worth the pain ...
the agony of involvement
will be earned by me
as soon as I heal,
when your memory doesn't appear
on another's face.

You were sent into my life,
an answer to a prayer.
I prayed for freedom
to be over the fright.
Now I know ... I know
I can now love without fear.

A fear that has consumed me,
taken love from my past,
transformed these loves
into shadows of a faded memory.

Fear's yoke has been broken.
At last, I am free.
Life's simple message
eloquently spoken
and so painfully learned.

Songs of Love

When I look into your eyes
as I speak to you of love,
you nod your head in agreement
… but I could not be heard.

Into green eyes, I try again.
You smile with understanding
so caring and so warm
you try so hard … but I could not be heard.

I change the medium
of my songs of love
from verbal to expression.
I know not where it landed
… for I could not be heard.

With love's pure strength
I show my inner feelings …
different levels of expression.
My heart grows weary
from beating alone
… for I could not be heard.

Something missing
between our beings.
Our souls could not connect,
for in the vacuum of a wounded heart,
the sounds of love are lost.
Your heart is encased
in hurt and fear
and can only hope
… to love.

My songs of love
are sad indeed,
… for I could not be heard.

She Never Cooked Lamp Chops

She Never Cooked Lamp Chops is about my decision to finally resign my position as chief "victim" and become accountable for me. The mantle of choosing the victim role is like living in a deep narrow well where the only sunlight comes from looking straight up and, even then, its intensity is diffused by the well's dark walls. When living in the dark at the bottom of this well, we victims expect benevolence from others to flow down to us just because of our self-induced state of helplessness. "See how pitiful I am? It is your responsibility to help me" is the message we yell to the world, a scream echoing off the well's dark and slimy walls.

Most victims have created their own deep wells of despair, as I created mine. Although it is hard to remove ourselves from this state of dependency and climb out, it really just requires a simple decision. All I had to do was change my thinking and quit expecting others to rescue me. I had to become responsible, simple but not easy. "Cooking my own lamb chops" in this poem is an analogy for my metaphoric climb out of the well of victimhood and into the sunlight of responsibility.

She Never Cooked Lamp Chops acknowledges my need to take care of myself and, finally, to stop expecting others to take care of me. I am now responsible for me. I am free…victim no more! Hallelujah! And with this responsibility, I now let others be responsible for themselves. I do not have to rescue, fix, or control another! Double hallelujah!

"Live and let live" as they say in 12-Step Programs.

She Never Cooked Lamp Chops

Being successful in my career
my expression of my love … my caring for her.
Amount of my paycheck was
the measurement of my affection.
   Yardstick of love.
Larger the amount … the more my love
more things to make her happy
to be happier and happier; yet we were not.

She never cooked lamb chops,
never made my favorite meal
no recognition of my accomplishments.
No respect paid to my success.
I expected her to be grateful … show me respect.
   Was she so blind?

But she never cooked lamb chops,
but I never told her what I wanted.
Mother always-made lamb chops;
why couldn't she?
   Unmet expectations gave way to anger.

Nor did I receive hugs, touch, understanding …
the emotional needs of life, I so desperately needed.
But then I didn't tell her what I wanted what I needed.
I wanted emotional closeness. She wanted it too.
We never told each other what we needed
   yet both were screaming …
   Understand ME!

No one heard, no one understood.
Too late now, that life is over.
I have to take care of myself …
   ask for what I need
   be thankful for what I get
   don't place that demand on another.
I have to cook my own lamb chops.

"Now where did I put that mint jelly?"

Celebration

During my mid-life crisis, I was a member of two singles groups. The one in Baton Rouge called itself "Celebration" and the one in Houston, Texas was called "SALT" (Single Adults Learning Together). The singles in the SALT group nicknamed our group and said with a chuckle, Single Adults Living Together.

With the Baton Rouge group, I still have many friends from those long ago years. This group of singles was like the clique you ran around with in high school, friends to hang out with who were always there for you and whose friendship remained even after leaving the group.

In both of these groups, we singles knew something was not working in our lives. There was some reason our marriages failed, and some reason we were single. Many of us felt discarded and unwanted. In this accepting environment, we were dedicated to learning about ourselves; trying to find out the lessons available from rejection's trauma; and maybe to, someday, commit again. (Someone once said that remarriage is the triumph of hope over experience!)

The poem, *Celebration,* is a dedicated to the many friends I experienced during those times and who helped me become who I am today.

Thank you, Celebration.

Celebration

Celebration, oh Celebration -
You named us well.
We are one together
union of wounded souls,
fellow travelers in life's journey.

Celebration, oh Celebration -
We share one common denominator
We are: mate less, single ... alone.
Instead of a curse of life,
we discover blessings from adversity.

As we hold together
singing praises to our creator ...
we dare to discover, who we are
daring to become.

Celebration, oh Celebration -
We are learning to:
love and be loved
nurture and be nurtured
risk again ... and maybe ... commit.

Celebration, oh Celebration -
We are learning to love ourselves
and wouldn't there be heaven on earth
when we all obtain the magic of self-love?

Celebration, oh Celebration
In our struggle to be become butterflies,
help us to give up our caterpillar life
we want to fly free in the soft summer's air

Celebration, oh Celebration-
help us to find our wings.

Epilogue – Celebration:

Footnote: Tom Lusk, a member of Celebration Single's group, made one of the wisest statements I ever heard and this understanding struck me as being incredibly true:

> "Wouldn't it be heaven on earth
> when all humans learn self-love?"

Tom, I think you're right.

Quiet Cul-de-sac

The house described in *Quiet Cul-de-sac* was located on Swift Creek in Kingwood, Texas. The purchase of this special house represented the high-water mark of my arrogance. When I bought this house, I thought I was someone. I had arrived! Success was mine...look how well I am doing!

When you do not like yourself, one way to attempt to compensate is by material processions and this house represented a failed attempt of hiding from the reality of my deep hidden unhappiness and insecurity. The more I acquired, the greater fear I had of losing it. The more success the world thought I had, the better I could hide my constant companion, misery. After all, how can one be miserable in that fine house?

The hollowness of my arrogance was revealed in this house on Swift Creek when reality struck. It was in this house where the wheels fell off my family life. My kids started their drug and alcohol addiction; my wife left me; and my business failed! All three atomic bombs went off at the same time, creating a lot of explosive and destructive energy. However, it was this cumulative effect of those tragic events which provided the energy I used to change; I turned the negative pronouncement of doom into the fuel necessary to change.

Quiet Cul-de-sac is about the house where the thin strands of self-respect finally broke and my world imploded. This tremendous trauma forced me to view myself differently. Because of those changes, my life is much more peaceful and rewarding.

Quiet Cul-de-sac

Swift Creek house – massive roof designed to impress,
visions of grandeur, stately, 'n regal
      color-coordinated interior,
      massive master bath,
      two car detached.
Loved at first sight; I knew I'd buy before entering.
      My dream house ... my dream house.
      Quiet Cul-de-sac ... country club neighbors

We moved in .. family of four.
New neighbors, schools, shopping, job
excitement, challenging, adventure
I had arrived ... high society –
eager to prove myself at my new position.
Invested myself in my company title. -
      Swift Creek house confirmed my self-worth.
      Quiet Cul-de-sac ... country club neighbors

Our family moved in with our past ...
Yesterday's problems never solved, hurts never healed.
Powder keg of emotions set to explode
      pressure cooker of family history boiling inside.

All bound together with family traditions,
rules, and rigidity from generations of prior families.
Family time-bomb, fuse set on adolescence –
      timer set generations ago.
      Quiet Cul-de-sac ... country club neighbors

Four years later, I walk through the ruins
still smoking embers of the recent explosions.
A blast - driving my family to the four winds,
twin destructive force of addiction and compulsive
behavior.

The ghost of our family still haunt that house,
yet, no one wants to return.
Memories are too fresh - too much pain and hurt.
      FOR SALE sign indicates change.
      Quiet Cul-de-sac ... country club neighbors

Lives forever changed by addiction and divorce.
Four wounded souls no longer together ...
          no longer a family.
Death of a family as we knew it.

This was my dream house ...
          and it turned out to be...
          nightmare house!

Quiet Cul-de-sac ... country club neighbors

Just a House

The next door neighbor on Swift Creek invited me to dinner one evening shortly after my separation from my wife. When I looked across her driveway towards my old house, now with the For Sale sign, a landmark for everyone to see my failure, tears welled up in my eyes as I grieved that loss.

My neighbor provided this insight for the poem *Just a House*.

Thank you, neighbor.

Just a House

"It's just a house ... not a home.
Nobody lives there.
You don't live there.
Your family doesn't live there. Nobody does."
Those words were true
spoken by a neighbor... a friend.

The house is empty ... No furniture.
No pictures on the walls.
No voices ... no people.
Only ghosts ... memories from the past
of what was and wasn't
and what happened there.

Memories flow in and out of my soul
in my mind through my aching heart.
Memories echo in this lonely house.
A desire by each member to love and to be loved,
wanting acceptance and understanding
all this wanting ...
wanting and not receiving.

We had a barrier which interfered with love,
attacking love like a cancer.
No intimacy. No sharing. No respect.
Afraid to express who we really were
what we were feeling
family self-worth was non existing
barrier caused divorce
.... addiction …
compulsive behavior.

Yet we all wanted to love …
and to be loved,
in that house ...
This house once our home but now is not.
"No one lives there. You don't live there.
No one lives there ...
it's just a house."

... of former spouses

Entering marriage is akin to walking backwards through the amusement park fun house. Marriage and fun houses are full of shadows, unexpected frights, and confusion. You haven't lived until you experience a fun house; you haven't lived until you experience marriage. My description of marriage fails miserably when expressed with the limits of the written word.

In graduate school at Texas A&M in Corpus Christi, Texas, I had a professor who made a profound statement. He said, "To have a successful marriage of forty years you have to go through five divorces!" I believe he meant that people in a long-term relationship change over the years; they develop new interests, new ways of thinking, and experience different pressures compared to when the first were married. People change over time and the relationship has to be flexible in order for people to grow in different directions.

In Louisiana, we experience hurricanes and it is the stiff oak trees that suffer the most while the willow and tallow trees bend with the wind and are not uprooted. Because of the winds of change, every once in awhile, couples have to renegotiate their marriage contract. A couple can be true to their vow, "Till death do us part" and still be flexible enough to allow change; this is healthy. Being ridged is not.

A friend has another interesting theory, "Marriages ought to be limited for only one year. Marriage should have a one-year period, an automatic termination, an expiration date. At the end of the year," according to my friend, "the couple then negotiates any changes needed in their contract and then decide if they want to re-up or not." Interesting theory.

During the course of a marriage, couples often do not realize they, their partner, and their relationship has changed; to their peril, they expect what was true in the past is true today. When confronted with the new reality requiring change, it is often painful and messy. When the relationship is stiff like the oak and there is limited flexibility, divorce often is the result.

… of former spouses celebrates my former life-mate with the forgiveness obtained from the realization, she and I were both trying the best we knew how. We resisted the changes and, like oak trees, suffered when the hurricane winds of mid-life crisis came we were ill prepared. Our "best" was ultimately inadequate, and divorce happened.

... of former spouses

There once was
'n never more shall be -
early life's love
beginning partner
hopes and dreams
anticipations and expectations.

Honeymoon bliss
Story book legends:
Happily ever after.
Love conquers all.

Society's myths – we believed
little by little ... caring overcome by
demands ... needs ... expectations
demanded from our spouse

Where is the moon you promised?
Fix my pain!
Make me whole!
Make me happy as you promised!
Fill my empty bucket!

Anger when not delivered
heavy burden – someone's else's happiness.

No more roses ... candle light
no smiles, no warmth, no sharing -
anger to breaking point
no communicating
death of the dream

Of former spouses ... people of worth
people we cared about
people we shared with
people we laughed with
people we suffered with
and then drifted apart ... forever apart.

Epitaph of Love

One of the suggestions I received from a divorce recovery seminar I attended was to have a "letting go" ceremony. There was much discussion over this suggestion. Some people planned to throw their rings across the river. One woman wanted to stomp on his grave, and some wanted to return something they kept but knew it meant something to their former spouse. I wanted my letting go ceremony to celebrate of what was good in our marriage in a respectful manner. I wanted to commemorate the positives in our failed relationship.

Under a shady oak tree in Rosewood Cemetery, Houston, Texas lays a special grave among many. It was at this site on a Sunday morning made fresh by a Saturday's rain, when I looked at the back of a gravestone and symbolically buried my twenty-year marriage.

Epitaph of Love was read to me, by me, commemorating many long ago memories…some good and some not so good.

My way of letting go.

Epitaph of Love

There once was 'n never more shall be ...
early life love extending into mid-life.
Now only exists as a memory, a shadow of the past
of how things were some time ago.
In the past, we were together dancing the dance of life
a pair in perfect sync ... with such grace 'n smoothness.
No one could see the pain, the anguish we were suffering.

We danced the dance...the dance of anger
a painful dance ...
a hurting dance but we knew the steps so well.
There was comfort in the familiar.
Being attached to another human being ...
shared last name, same house, same children ... the same bed.
Tomorrows belonging to us are forever destroyed.

Now is the time to put memories aside.
It is time to mourn, a time to remember,
feel the pain, the joy ... then forget.
Now is the time to bury our tomorrows ...
the future does not belong to us,
only two individuals, separated ... no longer joined.

I grieve what I have lost.
It's over. It is finished!
Time to put it to rest ... time to bury
to intern this relationship in the grave of yesterday,
to cover it with the cool moist earth ...
in the soil of nevermore.

I now commend this relationship to beneath the ground,
remembered by this tombstone marking this place
this occasion .. here we shall lie in the past.

As a couple of yesterday ...
it is over ...
it is finished.

Lover's Hill

I previously used the metaphor of buying a suit to a love relationship. Sometimes, as in that allegory, we pick out what feels right so we want to take it home on approval. Picking out a suit to wear is akin to when we are ready to deepen the commitment and send the invitation to our intended partner suggesting this commitment.

Lover's Hill is about someone who, when receiving an invitation to deepen our relationship, chose not to accept. I was left with a decision: continue with unsatisfactory status quo or end the relationship, lick my wounds, and move on.

Many life lessons had taught me I deserved the best a relationship could offer and I had the ability to return it full score. With this woman, I was proud I did not choose to settle, but burdened with a heavy heart …I chose to move on.

Lover's Hill

The top of lover's hill is covered with clouds,
with the valley hidden far below.
The soapbox derbies are at the top
ready to race ... to plunge into the unknown
in pursuit of the prize called love.

In the last race I entered, I suffered a horrible crash.
Since then my racer has been rebuilt,
new wheels and painted - shiny dark green.
On with the helmet and shoulder strap,
I am ready to race ... to risk,
springboard to personal growth.

The track down has many sharp curves and turns.
And in this race down lover's hill,
you, my dear, are the prize.
This soapbox derby is unlike my previous models.
This one actually has brakes!

No longer the head long rush, uncontrollable plunge
as so many times before.
Today will be slow, a leisurely drive.
As I coast down the mountain,
I stop at a roadside lookout
and view a majestic sight.
As far as the eye can see, the road curves down Lover's Hill
and far into the valley below, a journey of my lifetime.

When you decided not to race and didn't meet me there,
I sadly turned my derby around.
And with a heavy heart trudged up the hill,
not willing to continue without you.

This spot will be reached again
in another race with another prize.
I shall again pause,
survey, and plot my course.
Here I will fondly think of you
and remember the race
we never raced
but one
we might have won.

Epilogue – Lover's Hill:

Knowing what I know now and having experienced the contentment in my marriage with Penny, I'm glad the woman in Lover's Hill did not decide to race. Sometimes the answer "no" has a positive result, although at the time it sure did not feel like one.

Somber's Misty Dawn

I was staying in an apartment in New Orleans working on a large project for BP Refinery in Belle Chase, Louisiana. In the early morning murkiness between sleeping and awaking, while grieving the loss of a significant other, I awoke to this experience.

In this pre-awakened state, I wrote Somber's Misty Dawn to acknowledge the release I experienced when I shed this last tear of loss. It was my letting go ceremony.

Somber's Misty Dawn

A wetness
in the corner of my eye
brings me to consciousness
and, in somber's misty dawn,
awakens me
from dreams of you.

As the tear grows larger
I feel your tender presence.
No, this is a lie.
You are out of my system …
Yes, but not
quite
yet.

Residing between waking and sleeping
feeling love for you
then release
this tear finally escapes my eye.

Slowly with ever increasing speed
my tear flows down my cheek.
I feel release
as it leaves my face …
This last
tear
for
you.

When the moisture drop of love
finally wets my bed sheet below
only a single tear
was left
and now …
it too
has
been
shed.

Super Nova

Grief is a powerful motivator for me to sing the blues. A friend
called me the Bayou Bard and I liked that title. As you now know, it
is through poetry, this Bayou Bard expresses his melancholy.

I wrote Super Nova as I commuted between New Orleans and Belle
Chase when working on the BP project. This poem concerned the
same rejection whose tears you heard fall in Somber's Mist Dawn.

Super Nova

Twixt two earth seasons,
fall 'n winter
two traveling souls
crossed paths
in the peaceful intensity
of the black velvet void of existence.

She wouldn't lie here anymore.

Soul-stars are white hot
sparkling and twinkling
crisscross heavenly trails
creating a star ... a super nova
the wonder of the heavens.

She wouldn't lie here anymore.

Super Nova's brilliance
is witnessed by the universe
magnified by the vastness of space
and burns white hot 'n fast ... then quickly dies.

She wouldn't lie here anymore.

And from the deep woods,
an animal's wounded cry
who has lost his mate,
this cry is heard
across the heavens
and in the same instant
the super nova
has vanished ...

She wouldn't lie here anymore.

Magnolia's Blossom

Louisiana is blessed with its famous magnolia trees that remind the observer of early times when cotton was king and life in south Louisiana was simpler. The magnolia is the state flower of Louisiana and Mississippi. In the spring, the blossoms are fragrant and absolutely stunning with their beautiful blossoms of red, pink, purple, yellow but most striking of all white.

The poems *Magnolia's Blossom* and *... and the Lord,* are about lessons learned on the bitter altar of lost loves.

Magnolia's Blossom

A prayer for all seasons -
to love without fear.
Free from my bondage.
Let go of all else.
Focus on today
not ghosts of the past.

Love must flow
be equal and free.

When a love's not returned,
like Magnolia's sweet blossom
when picked in the morning
by late evening's shadows,
it withers and browns.

I feel very alone
so hurt and so hollow.
I deserve the best,
not second fiddle.

Someone to hold me
through the terror of the night.
To return my great love
free flowing and pure.

For a love not returned
will eventually die
'n buried with it
a single
Magnolia blossom
all withered
'n brown.

... and the Lord

*"And the Lord is close
to the broken hearted."*

A few remaining tears
are caught in my throat
waiting to be cried
wanting to be released.

I feel very close
to you, Lord
in my hour of grief
for my heart is heavy ...
this one was special.

She brought me so many gifts
many life's lessons
and because of this experience
much closer to thee.

Must I continue
to climb this spiritual mountain?
Must I seek to learn of thee
as a reflection of myself
in the caring face of another?

How many lessons are yet to be learned?
How many hurts are yet to be felt?

Life has now closed this beautiful door
and marked it with
the black Raven of Nevermore.

And I know God in His love
for me
will open another door
and then, perhaps another.

Just as the West Texas Mesquite bloom
heralds the beginning of spring
end of winter's bite,
I must begin again.

*"And the Lord is close
To the broken hearted."*

Lord, I want to be close to you ..
but isn't there an easier way?

Non-Occasion

When experiencing the death of a loved one, there is a tremendous amount of support given to the bereaved family and friends.

With divorce, a living death, seldom does the bereaved receive this needed support – cards are not sent, families do not meet for memorial, no gifts are given. The sufferer must go through a tremendous life upheaval often without the comfort so desperately needed.

Non-Occasion bemoans that distinct difference.

Non-Occasion

Divorce …
a non-occasion.
No one is invited,
only summoned.
No cake is cut.
No champagne served.
No rice is thrown.
No joy. No laughter.,
No promises.
No vows spoken.
No commitment. No future. No promises
Relatives not invited.

Divorce is similar to grave diggers
burying the dead
after the funeral.
Divorce buries the relationship
after the death.

The date only remembered
by the court records
and the participants.
No celebrations
only loss …
profound sense of loss.

Hopes and promises,
fade away into time,
are only memories
of the good and bad.

They are what remains
in this moment …
this non-occasion.
Not to remember …
only to forget.

Crowded Bed

A smart person learns from mistakes. A wise person learns from other's mistakes. I hope that you are smarter than I and can learn from my mistakes, or maybe you already have made them.

Crowded Bed and Twenty-Year Prayer is about life's painfully learned lessons in my 20-year marriage.

Crowded Bed

I gazed into your eyes
our hearts beat as one,
we understood our vows
the sum is greater than the parts.
Our souls would become as one
blending our lives in perfect harmony
losing our identity for the sake of the union.

This is what love is – two halves becoming one,
these expectations we believed.
Yet our marriage failed ... no more tomorrows ... why?

Nature believes in balance
two souls in perfect balance
so what was out of balance ... out of focus?
Why did our marriage fail while others thrive?

Our bed was too crowded!
Too many secrets ... too many pasts.
We were not our own person ...
melded together with expectations.
Repressed anger acted toward each other ... screaming,
"Give me what I did not get from Mommy and Daddy!"
No one heard ... no one understood.

These expectations ... our make-me-happy demands
stole the warmth from our union
forced our pain toward the wrong person
marriage doomed from the start
Not by you ... not by me
Not by your family ... nor mine,
Condemned by not knowing ... not understanding.
What an expensive price to pay
Twenty years ... expensive investment ... very expensive!

Twenty-Year Prayer

Many years ago our bed was brand new
all new ... just like our love.
Just broken in .. warmth 'n love ... sickness 'n in health
talked, shared, laughed, read funnies to our children
in our bed.
Ominous dark clouds on the horizon
Gulf 'tween the sheets ... grows wider
Prayer ... God answers prayers
I pray: narrow the gap, fill the void, decrease the gulf.

Twenty years prayer - gap gets wider, larger.
What's' wrong? No sharing, pain, distance
coldness turned colder, very cold, explosive anger
No response ... repulsive to my touch!
Why? Why? Why?

Bed is giant size, bigger that king ... miles wide.
What's wrong? ... No understanding.
What's wrong? ... No intimacy.
What could be done? ... Loss of sleep.
Wanting to know... Toss 'n turn.
What could I do? ... No sleep.

Find a solution, fix it, correct the problem - too late!
Move out! ... she says.
Leave me! ... she says.
No more! ... she says.
Ugly words ... hurting words.

Small apartment ... barren walls
Colder 'n lonelier, no one to share,
no one who cares, no one to touch
feel like yesterday's garbage, toxic trash.
Don't spend time alone – don't sleep in that lonely bed.
Dreams are shattered ...lifetime is over
"Never again" has new significance.
God answers prayers ... twenty-year prayer
and the answer is ... No.

Hurt 'n Anger Everywhere

Shortly after my 20-year marriage failed, I was very fortunate to find a divorce-recovery seminar at the Methodist Church on FM1960, Houston Texas. When I read the advertisement about the program, I knew I had to attend.

In the poem, *Hurt 'n Anger Everywhere,* these feelings are magnified and seen through my then wounded eyes.

Hurt 'n Anger Everywhere

Hurt 'n anger everywhere
divorce adjustment group -
does someone care ... understand?

Instructor speaks ... her voice soft, kind, caring.
What does she know? Can she help? Does she hold the key?
Want my wife back!
'Cause you're here ... it's over ... through, she says.
Words echo ... vibrate in the room, in my soul!
Want my wife back!

Hurt 'n anger everywhere
hurt of rejection ... hurt from guilt
hurt of "should of" ... hurt from "what if"
unfulfilled expectations ... incomplete dreams
Broken vows ... desertion - wondering what went wrong.
"Can't do things differently until you see things differently."
Want my wife back!

Eight week later - hurt 'n anger everywhere
controlled ... but not abandoned
understood ... but not lost
feelings are returning ... faces begin to glow
damaged pride recovering ... self-esteem emerges.

The wife's gone ... papers are filed
fight for the estate ... ugly ... life is over
long time ago – now a shattered dream
only memories ... remembered hurt
gut wrenching experience ... but strangely beautiful.
New friends ... thanks for the group ... someone cares.

We're not rejected material!

We are not "has beens" ...

No, we are "will be's"!

Epilogue – Hurt 'n Anger Everywhere:

In 1989, when I moved to Baton Rouge, I facilitated a similar divorce recovery classes entitled "Love Shock."

I knew from my own experience how powerful and helpful this program was to those who had suffered. This value was reinforced when one of the women attending this program had a fender-bender. She was very distraught because of this accident, not because they towed her car away but that her Love Shock Workbook was in the car and she was afraid she wouldn't get it back!

With this program, I felt I was giving back to others the blessing of the kindness and wisdom I received from my classes.

Used Parts

Someone gave me a piece of advice I took to heart. She said, "The secret of a good marriage is not finding the right person but *being the right person*." This turned out to be very true and as I discovered, we tend to attract our psychological twin. If we have a dysfunctional life style, guess what we attract and feel comfortable with?

When I develop healthier coping skills, a person, who is of like mental health, may be interested in me. If I am dysfunctional in my way of living, some fine woman may say to herself, "Nice buns, David but your maintenance is too high." If I live a dysfunctional lifestyle, a high maintenance person, guess who is attracted to me? Someone equally as dysfunctional. When I was so needy guess who I attracted? Someone who was also very wounded but her desire was to fix…we made a perfect match.

I knew I wanted to love again. I wanted another life-mate but this time I wanted something more. I wanted a healthy relationship. If there was a possibility of having a healthy lifestyle, I needed to think differently, to get better coping skills, and to change my attitudes.

"One man's trash is another man's treasure" as the old saying goes. Since my wife left me, she was the *dumper* in our relationship and I was the *dumpee*. In the spirit of the *dumpee*, I thought it would be a great costume for my first single's Halloween Party to show up as a person in a black plastic trash bag with a yellow caution ribbon warning "Dangerous Material" emblazoned all over it. (Sesame Street's Oscar had nothing on me.) This costume was the visual representation of what I was feeling, discarded trash, unwanted, yet part of me knew I was a worthy person. The Halloween costume represented what if felt like to the outside world but inside there was a burning desire to be better person.

Used Parts is about my suddenly being single but having the desire of something better and then discovering my own intrinsic value.

Used Parts

Used parts ... well broken in.
That's all I have
... all I can give
lots of miles on these used parts.

Many miles to travel
much life to live
before time ... my lifetime
recalls these used parts with fatigue

Used parts have been fully reconditioned
remanufactured by mid-life crisis.
Inspected 'n cross checked by experts
now guaranteed for life,
for a lifetime of use
one owner only ...
        these used parts of mine.

For sale to a person of worth,
quality person willing to pay
high price for these used parts ..
these used parts of mine ...
        they need a good home.

Soul Mates

Does a soul mate exist for everyone? Poets, like me, romantically expound on the reality of meeting our soul mates and living happily ever after. That myth causes much turmoil in love relationships, creating expectations another cannot possiblly fill. I sincerely doubt there is one person, out of all others, who is somehow divinely meant for each of us.

However, I have found humans have the ability to connect to another in deep and profound ways we do not understand but can enjoy. As my friend, Gloria Bockrath explains, "This is a Noah's Ark world. We are meant to live in pairs; it is a natural part of the human existence to find this connection." When relationships are successfully realized, it is quite remarkable. When absent, melancholy and despair are often the results of those now traveling single in this 2x2 world.

Soul Mates is celebrating the union of beings in a healthy and deeply spiritual experience.

Soul Mates

My daydreams are re-kindled.
My soul has learned
to fly.
Just by closing my eyes
my soul can now soar …
from purple mountain tops
with swift cold streams
into black holes
of night skies.

My imagination is unlimited.
Seeing into the night,
not with the vision of sight
seeing only with knowledge.

This close bond of humans
connects all …freeing us
forever from our dear
mother earth.

We tumble together
through the black holes
of the universe
playing tag with the stars
and leap-frog the Milky-Way.
My fear has no hold
for my bonds
are forever broken …
Release
is now
mine.

Songs in the heavens
singing praises
which connects
all soul mates
of the universe
with this god …
called Love.

Letting Go

This is an article I wrote in 1993 and published in the magazine Scrollin' ON The River

Life is a series of new beginnings and new endings. The night gives way to the morning light. A baby's fine hair is replaced by the dark of an adult, then sometimes replaced by bald jokes. There are natural processes that happen whether we want them or not, and nothing can be done to affect the final outcome. Unless we die young, we all have to face the reality of advancing years.

What is left is an opportunity for an attitude adjustment – a change of perception to fit current reality. In order for this natural dynamic to occur, a process has to happen called "letting go." To be able to press forward with the current reality of life and on life's terms, one must let go of the past, including the definitions and perceptions previously held which do not fit today's truths.

Although letting go is a common occurrence, sometimes for a variety of reasons, many choose to hang on, often with negative results, like being unable to let go of a shocking electrical cord. Emotional electrocutions are experienced whenever life's issues are not let go in a timely manner and the steady march of time insists on a psychic adjustment to a shocking new reality, yet we do not let go. By hanging onto a past reality, sufferers feel some control over what they really cannot control; the cost of accepting is too much. When this timing does not happen, sadness is increased and misery is our companion.

Sometimes what needs to be let go of is another person who the sufferer is reluctant to release. This is very common in the realm of romantic relationships or failed marriages. Some try to hang on to what isn't anymore, for the current reality is too painful for the jilted lover to accept. Anger is one of the ways of staying in a dead relationship. Even when the alliance has already been blessed with the last rites of divorce, some insist on staying anger at their now departed lover and with their tight grip on the past in an attempt to postpone the inevitable.

Relationship rigor mortis may have already set in, and one or both of the participants are still hanging on to its dead corpse with their anger, an all consuming rage which they cannot see for themselves but which is readily observable. Anger keeps the relationship alive by its powerful connection. To let go of the anger, they must release their past relationship, a painful reality which some are not ready to face.

A friend invited me to his 10th Annual Divorce party. I said, "Charlie...tenth annual...divorce party? When are you going to let go? How about having a new beginnings party?" No, he was not ready, and I wound up celebrating another divorce party with I'm-not-ready-to-let-go-of-my-anger-friend-Charlie.

When used correctly, anger can have positive results. But when it is the driving force in postponing the naturally occurring letting go process...devastating results can occur. The body stores this anger energy and that can result in stress-related diseases such as cancer, heart conditions, etc.

In addition, the people around the anger participants are also affected by the black cloud of red rage. One of the common denominators of parents of children in the juvenile court system is that the parents are fighting (married or not!). Do you want to have a positive effect on your life and the lives of your children? Let go and release the anger. *Negativity and happiness cannot exist in the same person at the same time.*

The first step in letting go is to acknowledge one is hanging on. If the relationship that is over and the anger persists, it is usually caused by obsessing over the lost partner. Although this may not be on a conscious level, anger is their way of maintaining the relationship, a connection now broken by time and distance. The solution would the obvious by allowing the letting go process to occur. Unfortunately, society does not have a letting-go ceremony for dead relationships. When a loved one dies, custom brings all the mourners together to a giant letting go ceremony called a funeral. Some divorce adjustment classes include an actual letting go ceremony, designed specifically for releasing a lost relationship.

Another letting go method is to write a letter. (Caution: Do not send to anyone, especially your ex!) This can be a good way of releasing pent up strong emotions. This letter can express anger or extreme sentimentalism or even both. Another effective method is a fake burial service, burying the relationship forever in the ashes of yesterday.

Open your heart and allow the Professor of Pain to enter, for being stuck is the worst part of the process. In the end, it's much easier to embrace the pain and allow the letting go process to happen than to continue being stuck in a dead relationship in desperate need of burial.

Part II - War

War has always held an intense fascination for me. As a kid, I loved to play with my army men and build plastic ship models, and balsawood airplanes. Shortly after their construction, as many little boys, I'd figure out how to blow them up.

I love reading about how battles were won or lost and the political ramifications of creating war or what happened afterwards. I enjoy reading about great heroism and comradeship created when men are in harm's way. If war didn't involve killing and men could just play war, it would be a great institution, but, unfortunately, with devastating reality, it demands death and suffering. Lots of suffering.

When walking in any long ago memorial battleground, I can almost feel the lost souls trying to communicate with me, not with the macabre evil of a horror story, but I sense they want me to know what it meant to them to sacrifice their life. They want me to know of the pain of dying and from their enlightened point of view they now know that war is so unnecessary. I feel this connection deeply, almost as if I was on the battlefield. I feel their fear. I see them bleed. I witness their death. I allow myself to become part of their suffering.

Tears form when I read stories of former enemies from the Soviet Bloc meeting U.S. servicemen who, up until the thawing of the Cold War, looked at each other through rifle sights. I see the healing associated with veterans who return to Vietnam, Iraq, or Afghanistan trying to reconnect with the lost part of themselves missing since they left that battlefield. I've seen old pictures of North-South Civil War reunions showing blue coated Yankees shaking hands with the grey beards of their old adversaries, a handshake of peace over the stone wall that marked the extent of Pickett's charge on that terrible day of July 4, 1863.

Should I have included this section on War when the first section is about love? Maybe it's the contrast between love and war, two completely different mindsets which inspires the mixing of these two diverse experiences. However, maybe when you read about war in this poetry, you will find under the thunder of guns, it is really about love.

The Eve of War

The Eve of War was written on the night before the beginning of the First Gulf War in 1990. I was hoping some other way would be found other than the destruction of war. History proves mankind again missed the opportunity and failed to prevent the killings.

When diplomacy fails, war results.

The Eve of War

On this, the eve of war,
visions of burned out tanks
charred and twisted guns
the smell of smoke
and broken young bodies.

On this, the eve of war,
a mother lights a candle
as silent prayer
on her tear stained lips
"Not my son, not my son."

On this, the eve of war,
I shudder as a flash of light
then explosive thunder …
jets crisscross darken skies.
Our young men try
to kill their young men.
We all count our losses.

On this, the eve of war,
as the body bags return home,
a mothers mournful cry,
a father's silent rage,
a young widow carries the child
he will never see.

On this, the eve of war,
my prayer, dear God
a nightmare only.
Let me awaken
to a peaceful
summer day with
sunlight shining down,
on this   … the eve …. of war.

One Last Warrior

When the First Gulf War began, the magnitude of what was happening across the globe weighted me down. I spent hours listening to CNN, reading newspaper accounts, and studying maps.

Those thoughts were on my mind when I went to bed one night and awoke in a cold sweat from the nightmare told in this poem, *One Last Warrior.*

One Last Warrior

A ray of light entered my room
and stood at the foot of my bed.
A woman emerged in angel attire
and showed me a wonderful dream.
On both sides of the trenches,
two opposing armies
forever laid down their arms.

Amidst the now silent guns
barefoot children threw
small white flowers in the air,
a mother's tear dries in her eyes.

Nation after nation banished war forever,
pledging never again to lift the sword!
Tears of joy ran down my cheeks,
living no longer with the threat of war
at last we can live as brothers!

The vision of light then spoke to me
as softly as my own mother's voice,

"This wonderful dream is the world's
to share. You may have it too.

One living sacrifice yet to be given
and this dream at last will come true."

"Take me," I shouted. "Take me!"
The shadowy woman shook her head,
        "No, not you.

This dream demands much, much more!"
"Anything, please anything," I begged.

"Give me one last warrior, one last death,
this world at last shall be free."
In the silence which followed
I knew the price to be paid.
Suddenly awake in my bed I shouted:

"No, no, not my son!"

Then this vision suddenly disappeared.
I was alone in my room.
And, at last, I knew the truth:
no matter what the rewards of war
or the cost of peace
I could not pay the ultimate price.

And as I cried myself back to sleep,
"No, no, not my son!," echoed in my head.

Soldiers' Cemetery

When I walked the Port Hudson battleground just north of Baton Rouge, Louisiana, I felt the spirits of the dead speaking to me. This is not a well-known battle and is only remembered by Civil War buffs and the locals who pass by this site. Even if only one body is offered in death as the sacrifice to the gods of war, this site has to be hallowed.

Soldier's Cemetery is the message I received from those entombed at this site; those bones want you to hear this message.

Soldiers' Cemetery

Hallowed ground ... field of honor
glory 'n country
white wooden crosses, row after row ...
thundering silence
of soldiers' cemetery.

"My eyes have seen the glory
of the coming of the Lord."

Songs they sang when goin' off to war.
Many never returned home
to witness a summer's sunset.

"When Johnny comes marching home again
hooray ... hoorah ..."

But Johnny didn't come marchin' home again ...
he died at Gettysburg, Cold Harbor, Shiloh,
Vicksburg, the Wilderness.

And with the cannon's roar
someone's young son
bartered his life
for this hallowed ground.

And a mother still sews a shirt
he will never wear.
And a father too proud to cry
plows a tear-soaked field.
And a young woman
still hears his voice a' singin'
as he carried her scarf off to war.

Old men's anger ... *young men's fight.*

Old men's pride ... *young men's blood.*

Could one cross in any row,
one young man's life among many,
satisfy the price of pride ...
the ransom for anger?

> *"Oh I wish I was in the land of cotton*
> *old times there are not forgotten ..."*

When Time Stood Still

When I first met Penny, who I would later marry, she encouraged many different ways of thinking about familiar knowledge. She challenged my love of the history and the iron will war imposes by her logic of disarmament. She challenged my corporate mind focusing on profit by satisfying world hunger. She challenged my abuse of the environment by her dedication to recycling. "If not me, who?" she would often say.

When Time Stood Still attempts to place life's seeming paradoxes into a work that provided clarity where, for me before, little existed.

When Time Stood Still

In a darkened room, one intense light shone on a green felt table.
Hushed voices, smoked filled room without clocks,
where time stood still.
The dealer, called Life, looked up from under his green visor.
He smiled as I entered long experience of spotting an easy mark.
"Back again, eh, hadn't seen you in here in a long time."
"Been awhile,"' I responded, "long while."
"No hard feelings about last time?" he asked.
"No, I learned a lot from the experience."

He shuffled the cards, then shuffled again, and began to deal.
"Are you ready to play?" I nodded my head in response.
Life's first card to me was from the External suit called: World Hunger.
In panic I looked at my hand, I didn't have an External card to play!
"Play the cards which I gave you," was the answer to my silent prayer.
I hesitated for a moment … 'n played
from the Internal suit called: Spiritual Hunger.

Life 's eyes riveted on my card, *"You never had Internal cards before."*
I looked Life in the eye, and then I knew,
Spiritual Hunger would beat World Hunger.
Satisfy the hunger in the souls of people
and the cries of the world's hungry would finally be heard.
Life then shuffled and dealt the card: Judgment.
Without hesitating, I trumped it with: Acceptance.
With a poker-face grimace, he played: Control.
My response was: Letting-go.
Card after card, trick after trick,
my Internal cards beat Life at his own game.

In silence Life stared at me, his scorn and contempt were apparent.
I felt the loving presence of my Creator's hand on my shoulder.

Life continued to stare, our eyes locked together.
A smile came over his face; for with his next card,
he anticipated victory. Life then laid down the ultimate challenge,
the deck's most difficult card!
Life now gambled the entire game on one card.
The card he played was: World Peace!
An icy sweat came over me,
my hands began to tremble
for I knew what card Life would play next.
If I could not trump,
Life would play ... **War!**

My lips began a silent prayer,
"Play your game", was the message I received.
The card I chose to play was Inner-Peace!

"Foul!" was Life's angry response,
"Inner-Peace can never beat World-Peace!"
With an angry flick of his wrist,
Life turned over the deadly card called .... **War!**

I felt my mouth move, I heard the words which came from my voice,
but I knew it wasn't me.
"Peace ... Peace begins with me," I quietly answered.

Life knew he had been beaten.
He slowly took off his visor,
turned his back on me,
and quietly shuffled out to the room,
... the room without clocks
... where time stood still.

If I Made the Rules of War

With the seriousness of war, I thought I'd end this section with some levity. If I Made the Rules of War is a spoof about my desire to change the nature of war, so instead of being harmful, it becomes a barrel of laughs.

With a little imagination and the world's permission, I could make war fun. Do you want to have fun and play war with me?

If I Made the Rules of War

If I made the rules, the rules-of-war
     what a wonderful war it'd be.
Nary a youth would give his life
     for our very own leaders would wage our wars
     leaving our boys in school ...
         if I made the rules ... *the rules-of-war.*

On a large hill, surrounded by bleachers this battle be fought,
     for we'd all want to see this fray.
We'd cheer with glee; the old men-of-war ...
     with all their pomp 'n pride.
Flags would fly; it'd be a sight to see;
     with varicose veins 'n large pot bellies
     as up 'n down this hill they'd charge.

On this field of honor, the warriors would be armed ...
     with pillows for battle axes 'n
     water balloons instead of swords!
Tickling would be encouraged, for then we all could laugh.
Guns, tanks, bombs or any loud noise wouldn't be allowed ...
         if I made the rules ... *the rules-of-war.*

As a fat president waddles up the hill,
     an ancient dictator swings his pillow at him.
When the president ducks, the dictators swings
     knocking the crown from a monarch's head,
     and the crowd goes crazy with laughter.
Once dethroned from King-of-the-Hill
     the vanquished would roll to the bottom,
     count to ten and then ten again ...
     'fore he became a new person.

After the battle the mother would serve
     a dedication feast,
     thanking these fine ole leaders
     for leaving their sons in school.

Lots of metals for these ancient warriors
      and their wonderful game called "war."

At the end of the day, these tired old adversaries
      would leave this field of honor,
      singin' songs of glory
      as arm 'n arm home they'd march,
      vowing to fight again …
           if I made the rules … *the rules-of-war*.

Part III - Death

Many people fear death for it is the ultimate of the unknown. We create many beliefs and myths concerning this inevitable adventure, the day our bodies cease to carry our life and our spirit leaves. There are many definitions, beliefs, and understandings which tend to comfort us when we lose a loved one or when we contemplate the day when our personal death sentence arrives, a date no one knows for sure.

People who fear death allow it to control their lives and fear dictates how they live out their remaining days. When consumed by the terror of the unknown, there is a tendency to attempt to manipulate the outcome by ritual compliance to certain beliefs others say will ensure life after death. This is comforting and may be correct but it can develop compulsive compliance to rigid rules, beliefs, and certain prescribed ways of behavior, all ensuring, as the myth or teaching goes, we will walk down the streets of gold as our reward.

Although this is comforting, will this understanding require us to give up something very precious...our freewill? The problem can become chronic when someone becomes obsessed with the fear of not doing it quite right or missing the mark and not fitting into the narrow eye of the needle required by some beliefs. For a life consumed by fear, there is no room for uncertainty, since doubt demonstrates the unpardonable sin, a lack of faith, a sure sentence to the pits of hell. How sad.

On the other hand, if death holds no fear, there is freedom to enjoy our time in the sun and look forward to this adventure of a lifetime, followed by our graduation ceremony into the unknown. When death holds not the terror of the unknown, doubt can be the tool of learning, the attendant of discovery, providing the freedom to explore. Doubt does not change the truth but brushes away the underbrush to reveal reality. The ultimate truth about death and what happens next, no one really knows for sure. The dead are not speaking and our knowing would spoil the surprise.

My very good friend, Ken Harris, who now is on the other side of the veil of death had some unique explanations concerning life. He called our bodies our "space suits." Ken explained, "At birth we are issued a space suit to explore life. These space suits are all somewhat different. I was issued a white male suit and that suit has a certain limitation on how I experience life and at my age I now begin to feel it is wearing out. Had I been issued a female space suit, I would experience life as a female whose understanding would be certainly different than this male body I call home."

He continued, "These space suits have certain strengths and definite limitations and the luck of the draw dictates which space suit was issued. Some might be made well or some have malfunctions plaguing them from birth."

Thinking about Ken and his space suit theory, much of how we define ourselves is based upon what space suit we have, where the suit was raised, and what climate (political and culturally) it was raised in. If I am tall and athletic, my life will be different than if confined to a wheelchair. If I am raised in poverty this space suit experience is vastly different than if I am raised in the lap of luxury. Maturity dictates and provides the opportunity to give up space suit limitations and definitions to see ourselves, not in the physical realm, but as our life-spirit encapsulated in a space suit, our bodies.

Using that definition, isn't it interesting how we tend to define ourselves and label others based upon what space suit was issued? Race, gender, size, age, and sexual ordination are all definitions the world provides and we adopt. Often these labels are in flagrant disregard to the spirit housed within. Are we not much more then these definitions of our space suits?

Death provides us with personal gestalt. (I love using that word for it makes me feel so intelligent.) A Gestalt is a German word not readily translated into English. According to Merriam Webster, a gestalt is "…a structure, configuration, or pattern of physical, biological, or psychological phenomena so integrated as to constitute a functional unit with properties not derivable by summation of its parts." Rephrasing this definition, a gestalt is seeing a system differently.

When humans first launched themselves into the vast reaches of space, we turned around and took a picture of the earth. With this picture of our shining blue sphere surrounded by the vast inkiness of black space, we experienced a gestalt: seeing this image, humans knew earth differently than ever before.

When we die, many believe we will experience another gestalt; we will be able to see ourselves and others not as defined by the limits of our space suits but as actual spiritual life forms. How exciting.

Ken also had another unique point of view. He told me, "We are in stage two." When he saw the puzzled look on my face, he continued, "Before we are born we were in stage one and when we die we enter stage three." That description fit with the reality I now enjoy.

So the poems in this section are dedicated to my loved ones and many friends who have already experienced death and eagerly await my arrival. These poems are written while living in stage two in contemplation of the excitement and wonder of stage three.

Death can Only Weep

When disconnecting the TV set from the power outlet what happens? Yes, the picture goes out. Is the signal still there? Of course, for the problem is not the signal but the receiving device, the TV. Maybe death is just the loss of the receiving device; the signal is still there but we cannot see for our receiver is broken, a space suit malfunction.

Some think that death is really just an illusion that we cannot yet understand. Death can Only Weep contemplates that idea.

Death can Only Weep

There will be a day...
the day I die.
Not unlike the day
I was born.

At birth I began to die
and it will be at death
I will begin to live.

For it is only at death
we are released
from the illusions
of this life.

Just as the passage
from the womb
confronts us with life
in another dimension,
death brings the world's
shadows into focus.

For death can never be an escape
for it is not life
where the problem lies.

Living is a joy ...
and the opposite
is in the eye of God ...
For nothing
He did not create
is real.

The past just slips away
replaced with everlasting quiet.
And at life's death
we will make the final discovery.

We were not created to die.
We can laugh at death
for it is not real …

            … death can only weep.

Final Adventure

I would like to invite you to my graduation ceremony. It will be held on the day I die and if you are attending my good-bye service, you are still living and I am now departed. If you are one of those attending this graduation ceremony, I want you to realize... *"I now know!"* I now have ultimate knowledge of what is beyond the gray veil of death. I now know... *You do not!*

When I think of death, I ask myself a powerful question, producing profound realizations. This magical question, if we allow it, can become a wonderful stress reducer for any of life's traumas including the query into death...our death.. The question to ask yourself when trauma hits is this, "I wonder what I will learn?"

The poem, Final Adventure, is how I view my death; when with glee, I shall pass from this life to the next. I'm not too excited about the dying part of death but that in itself will be an adventure, a lesson to learn —maybe painful, maybe not, but something each of us has to experience. Maybe our personal appointment with the Grim Reaper may turn out to only be grim...to those we leave behind.

Final Adventure

Excitement of living, feeling the sun on my back,
the wind in my hair, and the smell of sea breezes,
enjoyment of one moment in time.

Living life as it was intended
with the intensity of love
and freedom of spontaneity.
Fully embracing all the joy and sadness
life can provide.

At the end of my journey
there is the final door
the omega of life,
death ... the final adventure.

A darkened room
is frightening to a child,
as is the passage from one life to another.
And there can be one answer to my quest,
one journey not yet taken.

Returning home to my creator
to learn what is left to know.
Answers to unanswered questions
death ... the final adventure.

Those who are left behind can say:
"He embraced the celebration of life.
His laugh was hardy. He knew love well.
He now resides at journey's end".

I shall have lived my life fully,
if you can carve on my stone:
People respected him.
Little children loved him.
And he was true to himself.

When I depart from flesh and blood
which entraps my inner spirit
to the living ... I send my farewells
and
death ... the final adventure.

Move...Stop

What happens when our earthly space suit of life no longer functions and the last grain of sand falls through our hour-glass of life? When the seconds finally run out of our life's clock? What happens to the picture and sound on the TV when the plug is pulled and the power is gone? We are pronounced dead. *But are we?*

The TV signal is still alive but our receptor has ceased functioning; it is dead and no longer able to pick up this signal. On that final day when the doctor shakes his head and offers condolences to our family, what happens to our spirit? Could it be like the TV set, our signal is still there awaiting another receptor to bring it back to life?

The poem Move...Stop does not contemplates this intense question but instead wonders about our relationship with the disappearing sand and the ticking of our watch marching toward our day with destiny.

Move...Stop

The second hand on my watch
marks time's passing.

At each stop a new second begins.
Each second is another to enjoy.
Each second is closer to death.

Move...Stop.
Move...Stop.
Move...Stop.

My hour glass has a limited
amount of sand.
When each grain drops
the amount left decreases.

How many grains do I have left?
How many seconds remain?

Move...Stop.
Move...Stop.
Move...Stop.

Unless interrupted by breakage
releasing the sand at once,
I have a predetermined
amount of seconds to count
of life yet to live.

Each day I move closer and closer
to that day...
the day my sand runs out
the day seconds are exhausted.

Before my terminal death sentence
is carried out
I plan to live as a youth
enjoying the infinity of life
like an endless barefoot summer.

Move...Stop.
Move...Stop.
Move...Stop.

Field of Buttercups

When one of my classmates from E. C. Glass High School died in 1990, his passing, how he died, and how he spent his life caused many of his remaining classmates to shake their heads in judgment and left all of us with unsettling feelings.

Field of Buttercups is my pondering of his death and my saying good-bye to this classmate. A youth, like me, who once breathed the breath of promise and experienced the fog of disappointments and was no longer capable of attending the next reunion.

Field of Buttercups

Under the shadow of the president's monument,
a brilliant field of buttercups
consumes the sun's intensity
of late summer's afternoon.

All the mourners meet at the grave,
resting place of our classmate
buttercups' beauty
contrasts with the pale grey of death.

Bowed heads shed tears of remorse,
funerals are for the living
where we can share our grief.
The sharp knife of death has cut another soul
from the fabric of our lives.

We all breathed the same air
saw the same sunsets
drank from the same fountain of dreams
and in the innocence of our youth
thought life unending.

We laughed and cried with him,
who's life is now tragically ended
in the beginning of his prime.

He died as he was born
without earthly possessions
and in the company of strangers.
It is not for us to understand or forgive,
only accept; his death was his way,
for his reasons, in his time.

As I walk this field of buttercups,
I feel a sudden rush of air
and I know it is him,
returning with gifts for the living.

For on one side of the coin of life
we witness the tragedy of death,
on the other, the blessings of grace.

As the last of the earth is shoveled over his box,
a part of me dies with him
but with the cry of a baby's birth,
another part goes on.

Ole Dogs 'n Babies

When I was attending Texas A&M graduate school in Corpus Christi Texas, I attended a Twelve-Step meeting where one participant talked about a funeral he just witnessed. When this participant spoke, he did his best to recreate what he learned at the funeral. It was so powerful I attempted to immortalize it in this poem.

Maybe this man's death was the entire reason for his living, to provide a powerful lesson to those who were left behind. Hopefully, I've paid the required tribute to this man's death and what it may mean.

Old Dogs 'n Babies is my recounting this story about an old man's tragic life who was once with us but now is no longer here.

Ole Dogs 'n Babies

The room was quiet, dignified and refined
        only muffled voices could be heard.
        Gathering of the living
        honoring the departed, paying required respects
        demanded by society
        to the body now lying before us.

As I surveyed this funeral gathering
        of all his relatives and friends
        no one was wailing, crying or mourning
        all were quiet and still.

Four score and four this man been living,
        now not a tear was shad.
        He died as he lived, as tragic a story
        without nary a friend to his name.

No one ever knew him
        'cept ole dogs 'n babies
        for them he'd allowed to get close.
        Ole dogs 'n babies wouldn't harm him
        disappoint him, or reject him,
        nor judge him nor demand him;
        these he could love without fear.

No one knew this now dead man;
        he'd not let them get very close
        not the daughters he raised,
        the preacher who buried him,
        or the woman he took for a wife.

The real tragedy of this now wasted life
        displayed by the service I witnessed,
        was here was a man who walked on this earth
        and never knew himself.

At Rest

While attending the funeral services for Penny's mother in Johnson City, Texas, I witnessed a startling contrast. After the funeral services, I was asked to entertain two little girls at the gravesite ceremony so that they would not disturb the solemn proceedings. This I gladly did, giving me something to do and momentarily obliterating my own sorrow. I took these two beautiful children to a grassy area about 50 feet from the gravesite.

It was in early spring with a gentle coolness in the air and flowers were in full bloom. The Hill Country of Central Texas is blessed every spring with the most lavish display of color making a canvas that would make Van Gogh jealous. In every field, there are acre after acre of brightly colored flowers ~~of blue and orange~~, called Bluebonnets and Paint Brushes. Tourists come from many states just to marvel at this breathtaking blue and orange display of beauty.

These two little girls were picking these beautiful flowers, making bouquets, and mimicking the solemn posture of the adults they witnessed as they reverently placed these flowers on a stranger's grave. With their brightly colored dresses, curls over their foreheads, these two little girls were oblivious to the pain their adult relatives were experiencing.

Several times over this funeral weekend, I heard mournful statements made by Penny's father who had just lost his wife. He would say to anyone within earshot but unconcerned about who heard; obviously, he was speaking mostly to himself. Those mourning statements echoed in my head and were in harsh contrast with the innocence of the two little girls making bouquets and giggling as they pretended to honor the grave they stood upon.

In the poem *At Rest*, I contrast the joy of innocence of these two little girls with the grief my father-in-law expressed.

At Rest

Two very young girls,
all curls and Sunday best
picking wild flowers
and gently placing them
on a stranger's grave.
"Why did she have to go now?"

Wild flowers...
Bluebonnets of
yellow, blue, and orange.
"Fifty one years with her, what am I going to do?"

Not old enough to ponder death
or seek to understand,
innocence has sheltered these youths
from the reality of this world's
questing "Why?"
"She' at rest but I am not."

Muffled mourners' sobs
mingles with the distant preacher's voice,
mumbling unimportant words
only comfort for the ones left behind.
"I can be brave in the daylight; it's the nights I fear."

The mourners pay their last respects.
The casket is lowered into the ground.
The sun will rise tomorrow; life will go on.
"She's at rest but I am not."

Two young girls with golden curls
are gently hugged up by their mothers.
As the sun of early Texas spring fades, they return home.

And in their absence, the old man is left
with his profound loss.
He softly mumbles to himself...
"She's at rest but I am not."

Baseball in Heaven

As a youth, I loved to play baseball. I was a very poor hitter but I loved to pitch. I loved putting that old ball into the tightest corners of the plate and feeling the thrill when the batter swung and missed or when the umpire called…"Strike!" My crowning baseball achievement in little league was pitching a no-hitter.

All my coaches agreed, I would have had a brilliant baseball career and had kids collecting my face on baseball cards if it was not for the sad tragedy I suffered. What was this tragedy you ask…a tragic lack of talent!

If you are alive and I am not, turn your head toward the heavens, and listen real closely. Can you hear the excitement of the crowd and the voice of the announcer? Can you see the green of the infield? Can you hear the crack of the bat, the smell the leather gloves, and the taste of a hotdog in your hand?

Baseball in Heaven celebrates the game in the sky on my special day.

Baseball in Heaven

There's baseball in heaven.
I just know 'tis true,
because on the day I die
there'll be a double header.

There's a ballgame in heaven
'n upon my death
It'll be me upon that ole mound
hurling for the Heavenly Angels.
I'll be throwin' strikes
'n doin' pick off plays.
My ERA will be the envy.

So on the day I die have a party
    at the old ballpark
     'n do this in remembrance of me.
All gather at pitcher's mound
    'n right after Amazing Grace
    say a few words in eulogy
    'n call this talk,
     the *Sermon on the Mound.*

Then lift your eyes high unto the stars
'n strain' your ears real hard.
For above the noise
    of the earthly din,
    the heavenly host
    can be heard.

At this game in the sky,
    the crowd will be screamin'
    at the top o' their lungs
    actually goin' mad with glee.

These are the fans
    of the Heavenly Angels
    'n the pitcher on the mound
     will be me!

Epilogue – Baseball in Heaven:

Since I wrote the poem, *Baseball in Heaven* in 1990, I have since followed my grandfather and my dad in their love of tennis. Both were avid players and played semi-pro tennis in Florida.

Now those of you who played tennis with me know I am not close to that exalted ability, but I think my grandfather and dad will have a tennis match waiting for me when I arrive. Since I do not play singles, I wonder who will be our fourth.

So, at my funeral service you may not then hear the heavenly host because I will be pitching the next day. I know on the day I call it quits, I'll be serving aces to my grandfather and dad.

I can't wait.

Keep the Fork

This submitted to Spiritual Stories Archives on January 10, 1999 by John Gardiner.

"There was a woman who had been diagnosed with cancer and was told… to start making preparations to die… So she contacted her pastor and had him come to her house to discuss certain aspects of her final wishes.

She told him which songs she wanted sung at the service, what scriptures she would like read, and what she wanted to be wearing. The woman also told her pastor that she wanted to be buried with her favorite Bible.

Everything was in order and the pastor was preparing to leave when the woman suddenly remembered something very important to her. "There's one more thing," she said excitedly.

"What's that?' came the pastor's reply.

"This is very important," the woman continued. "I want to be buried with a fork in my right hand."

The pastor stood looking at the woman not knowing quite what to say. "That shocks you doesn't it?" the woman asked.

"Well to be honest, I'm puzzled by the request," said the pastor.

The woman explained, "In all my years of attending church socials and functions where food was involved … my favorite part was when whoever was clearing away the dishes of the main course would lean over and tell you to keep your fork. It was my favorite part because I knew that something better was coming. When they told me to keep my fork, I knew that something great was about to be given to me. It wasn't Jell-O or pudding. It was cake or pie. Something with substance. So I just want people to

see me there in that casket with a fork in my hand and I want them to wonder 'What's with the fork?' they will ask. Then I want you to tell them, 'Something better is coming so keep your fork too.'"

The pastor's eyes welled up with tears of joy as he hugged the woman goodbye. He knew this would be one of the last times he would see her before her death. But he also knew that the woman had a better grasp of heaven than he did. She knew that something better was coming.

At the funera, as the mourners viewed the body … the pastor heard the question over and over again, "What's with the fork?" He only smiled. During his message, the pastor told the people of the conversation he had with the woman shortly before she died. He also told them about the fork and about what it symbolized to her.

The pastor told the people how he could not stop thinking about the fork and told them they also would not stop thinking about it either. He was right. So the next time you reach down for your fork, let it remind you… there is something better coming."

My Mother

Jean Aevelyn Barbara Carlson Earle was the woman I was proud to call my mother. I would describe her 94 years in just two simple words: *giving and laughter*. Her gifts to all people came from her large heart; she loved to give. She also always found a way to laugh even in her most bitter disappointments; her smile was infectious. She constantly found ways to give to others and bring joy to those who needed a smile or kind word. When I worked at Louisiana State University, I took liberties with this appointment and made her a diploma recognizing her completion of a Master's Degree as a Jollyoiogist, I should have made her a Ph.D.

As she grew older her mind began to lose its sharpness, but her desire to give always remained intact. When I would visit her and aske what she wanted to do, she would look incredulously at me, for I should know by now, "I want to go shopping." Now shopping for my mother was different. It was not for herself but for everyone else. We would head for all the bargain stores, thrift shops, and nearly new boutiques she knew so well. She would fill her basket with items she was convinced would make another happy. Often her gifts did not meet another's expectations but as the old saying goes, "It is the thought that counts", and Jean Earle counted.

For many years, she did hat shows. Jean had a collection of hundreds of old hats and she would take them to any organization who invited her. Sometimes it would be a church Sunday school class, a mental health clinic, rotary meeting, orphanage, or garden club. She would show a hat, and then tell a little story about the history of hat or how it was made, the significances of the feathers, and explained the style in relation to its era.

Ultimately what made the show so delightful was she gave each person a mirror. After explaining each hat, she would pass out the hat to the participants. Now what is the common reaction when a person receives a strange hat and a mirror? You guessed it. All participants would put the hat upon their head and look at themselves in the mirror. The laughter began slowly but by the time a few hats were passed out even the most depressed person would view themselves in these various silly hats and laugh.

The first time I experienced her doing one of her Hat Shows I did not want to attend to hear about some dumb old hats but my mother was hard woman to say no to, so I reluctantly went. I attended thinking I could be her moral support. She started her discussions so seriously, but I was surprised when people began to laugh. I became defensive and protective of my mother and thought, "How dare they laugh at my mother!" Then I looked at Jean and saw the sparkle in her eye. I immediately knew then what her hat shows were all about; she was practicing her gift as a Jollyologist. She proudly called herself the *Happy Hatter*. With this unique gift, she made others laugh.

Jean wrote her own obituary dedicated for those she loved and left behind when her spirit departed this earth. This was her wish and even as her last breath escaped her well worn body; she wanted to make another's life better than it would been had she not lived. I think she was successful as her life was full of meaning.

It is fitting that the next poem is included in this section for it not only sums up her life but a reassuring attitude toward death.

This is Jean's wish

To Remember Me – I Will Live Forever
Robert Noel Test

"When on a certain day, at a certain moment,
a doctor determines that my brain has ceased to function,
and for all intents and purposes, my life has stopped,
PLEASE , do not attempt to instill artificial life into a tired body.
And don't call this my death bed.
call it my great adventure.

Give my sight to a person who has a need to see the sunrise,
to a person who loves life and will enjoy the color of nature,
and who will use the eyes to help others.
Give my heart to a person whose own heart has caused endless pain.
Give my blood to a teenager who has had an accident.
Give my kidneys to one who may need a weekly visit to a machine.
Take my bones, and every muscle, fiber, and nerve in me
and make then grow for a child in need.

Burn what is left of my body and scatter the ashes at a party.
I would be thrilled to be taken on another ride on the Staten Island Ferry.
If you must bury something,
let it be my faults, my weaknesses, and all my prejudices.
Give my sins to the devil.
Give my soul to God.
When you remember me, do it with a kind deed.
Remember me with a kind word to someone who needs your concern.
Remember to laugh every day.
If you do all this that I ask, then I will live forever...
Thanks be to God."

We found this poem in her keepsake box written in her handwriting. At
the end, she signed this poem with...

"Best wishes from the Happy Hatter."

Epilogue:

One of Jean's most ardent desires was for her now departed body to be of some use to someone else. She wanted her organs harvested for another's use and she willed her body to science. Sadly, the stringent requirements for this wish are for the body to weigh more than one hundred pounds. With the ravages of age, she lost significant weight and at her death, she did not qualify for her last request.

Just before her funeral, we did have her remains cremated. One thing she wanted was for the family to have a reunion in her home city of New York where the family would say goodbye to Jean. She also requested to have her earthly remains scattered off the back of the Staten Island Ferry. The family is not ready to grant Jean her last request and have this ferry boat ceremony for then her last physical presence will no longer with us.

At Jean's service in the Quaker Memorial Methodist Church, we all said our last goodbyes and vowed, as she requested, to let go of her "faults, weakness, and prejudices." To celebrate her life during this service we all knew how best to do this…we held a hat show… right there in church! All of the family, men and women, wore one of Jean's hats. In these old-fashioned women's hats, we all looked ridiculous, we all laughed at one another, and we all remembered the *Happy Hatter*, our mother.

Mother laughed her way through life giving to everyone she met. She was the Johnny Appleseed of love, leaving seeds of laughter to grow in others. This is her legacy. This is what gave her life meaning. This is the Mom I love.

Closing Thoughts

Death is the final adventure. When I leave this earth heading for our eternal reward, I know I can only take two things with me on this journey. Out of all of my processions, titles, awards, recognition, degrees, validations, victories, and math whiz cards, only two things can accompany me.

I leave to you, my loved ones, perhaps with your eyes moistened by remembrance, a lifetime of the love I gave and the tokens of material processions expressed in my will. As imperfect as my love was to you, I hope you are now better person because of my love or perhaps you are saddened by its incompleteness. As imperfect as it is, my parting gift to you is the love I left with you.

What I will take with me when I die is the love I received. This love is the sum total of my time on earth, the love I received from my mother's first lullaby, my father's first prideful hug through to final tears of sadness by the mourners regretting my departure. I am richly rewarded by this love I received from you, cherish it, and be comforted by its presence as I journey forth into the unknown. St. Peter will know it's me by the tremendous amount of love I carry onto the streets of gold.

The second treasure I will take with me on my final adventure is what I learned, life's lessons. Life is a unique learning opportunity and is the reason I came here in the first place in my spacesuit you call, David. Death now allows me to see my life from a different viewpoint enabling me to be thankful for the lessons I learned and realized what I do not know, lessons available but I chose not to study, wisdom yet to be acquired.

At my 50th class reunion, I realized there were many classmates I really did not know and I wanted desperately to lock the doors not allowing anyone to escape back to their normal lives. I wanted a chance to learn to love them. This realization was another insight on what I now understand. All the lessons I have learned so far on earth and I am now taking with me can be simply summed up and it is this realization I leave as my final gift of inheritance.

My entire time on earth has been a lesson on how to love.

So all of you who witness this event, hold me gently in your thoughts:
- I am thankful for having the opportunity to have lived life.
- Perfect love was neither given nor received but it was the best we knew how. I am grateful for those whom I love and thankful for the love I received from you.

And it is at death, I will begin my next learning experience. It is my desire to leave this earth, surrendering my earthly space suit, and be cremated with a...

...fork in my hand.

Amen.

Acknowledgements

When I wrote the book, *What To Do While You Count To 10*, it was Penny, my bride and partner of over 20 years, who was my original editor (See, I did finally get the girl!) It was her confidence in my writing that gave me the will to pursue my dream of writing. She deserves as much credit for the creation of that book as I do. I will be forever grateful for her effective feedback and support.

Ever since our dating days, she was always interested in my poetry and is the subject of many of my poems. Without her influence, confidence, and her undying support of my abilities, I would not have attempted the major undertaking of writing the series of three books included in the Live Poets Society.

Many other people have encouraged my publishing these poems that I would be remiss if they were not included. The first group includes my two children, Garrett Earle and Ginger Earle. They were many times the source of the inspiration for writing. If it were not for what we experienced together, often associated with the pain of learning, I would be devoid of the fertile soil needed for emotional poetry. Thank you, children, for teaching your dad.

In this same vein, I want to acknowledge my ex-wife, Sandi Earle. We spent 20 years together and as I jokingly call her, "my starter wife." I could not be the person I am today without that experience. I apologize for all the mistakes and pain I caused her, but I am tremendously appreciative for the life we shared even under those trying circumstances. I once told her, after our divorce, due to changes I made working to improve me, I was now a "recovering ass-hole." She quickly retorted, with all of the cutting fury an ex-spouse is entitled, "I doubt the recovering part!"

During my mid-life crisis when I was trying to learn how to live a peaceful life without the chaos I was so accustomed …and often creating, a couple of girlfriends encouraged my offering this poetry to a wider audience. The first is Terri Bonde. After watching the movie, *Little Shop of Horrors*, she told me that I had so much creativity that I could write a story like that in "one afternoon." That thought has stuck in my mind and although I tend to discount her confidence in me, her assurance stills tempers the depth of my uncertainty.

Joan McKenna was instrumental in believing in my abilities and many times asked when I would publish my writings. She is a substance abuse counselor and I was enthralled with her abilities to relate to those in crisis. She is one of the people who inspired me to completely change my career and enter the mental health field. So, Joan, here are the books you asked for, I hope I lived up to your expectations.

Cindy Cook was another Celebration friend who always wanted me to read her my poetry. She was also a poet so we often shared what we wrote and one time actually combined her poem and mine together like a duet.

I have a long time friend, Kimberly Coburn, who also encouraged me toward entering the mental health field. She often suffers depression, and one night she showed up at my house throwing pebbles at my window to wake me, seeking the understanding she needed at the moment and escape from her constant companion, melancholy. Somehow, when I listened to her and adopted a non-judgmental attitude it helped her through her various crises. From that experience, I knew I must have the gift of understanding and I knew then I must follow my bliss. Because of what I learned from her, I decided to attend graduate school at Texas A&M University for mental health counseling.

Her story would not be complete without telling what happened on one dreary Monday afternoon when she was depressed. She called me and said that I was to meet her at Sicily's Pizza for a party at 6:30. This was, as she called it and "un-party." I was tired and the last thing I wanted at that time was a party. "No," she insisted, "I am calling all my friends and you will attend. No excuses." Reluctantly, with her insistence, I attended.

A number of people from our singles group halfheartedly showed up, all with pained faces for having to change their plans for a quiet evening and attend this quickly arranged and desperate party. Many brought their kids and Kimberly brought a chocolate cake. The kids were excited to see the cake. I made some sarcastic remark about, "That is the last thing I want to after eating pizza." She said "Oh, no, this cake is special; we will eat it now!" The kids went wild with excitement, dessert before the meal, how wonderful.

When we looked for a knife and plates to begin this backwards meal, Kimberly again interjected her will. "No, do not use a knife; this is how you eat this cake." With that explanation, she reached her hand deep in the cake and purposefully put a big bite in her mouth that resulted in having lots of chocolate all over her face. For a moment in shocked horror, we stared, but then our own suppressed inner children took over and we also grabbed handfuls; soon covered with chocolate with big smiles on our face.

She later told me this was her way of fighting her demon depression, doing exactly opposite of what the depression was telling her. Her depression wanted her to stay home, isolate from others, and feel sorry for herself but instead, she forced herself to do the opposite. This is a story I tell others who suffer from depression and is a great way to manage the blues.

Kimberly's greatest contribution to this book is her suggestion to contact Laci Talley, to be the editor for this series of books. Laci turned out not only to be an excellent editor, to whom I'm eternally grateful, but her perception of the change process necessary to seek the inner peace made my writings come alive with understanding. She also would not let me to indulge in any self-deflating statements that tended to diminish the power of my writings. Our combination created a connection to convey this emotional poetry into something ~~you will enjoy reading~~ *to enjoy*.

No acknowledgement can be complete without thanking the smiling confidence from my business associate for many years and now good friend, Jan Zeringue.

I have a business associate, Jeff Gorter, who found out my interest in writing and now calls me the *Bayou Bard*. I hope I can live up to the title.

Proof

Made in the USA
Charleston, SC
08 March 2014